D1628455

ROUGH GUIDE STAYCATIONS
NORFOLK & SUFFOLK

YOUR TAILOR-MADE TRIP
STARTS HERE

Tailor-made trips and unique adventures crafted by local experts

Rough Guides has been inspiring travellers with lively and thought-provoking guidebooks for more than 35 years. Now we're linking you up with selected local experts to craft your dream trip. They will put together your perfect itinerary and book it at local rates.

Don't follow the crowd – find your own path.

HOW ROUGHGUIDES.COM/TRIPS WORKS

STEP 1

Pick your dream destination, tell us what you want and submit an enquiry.

STEP 2

Fill in a short form to tell your local expert about your dream trip and preferences.

STEP 3

Our local expert will craft your tailor-made itinerary. You'll be able to tweak and refine it until you're completely satisfied.

STEP 4

Book online with ease, pack your bags and enjoy the trip! Our local expert will be on hand 24/7 while you're on the road.

BENEFITS OF PLANNING AND BOOKING AT ROUGHGUIDES.COM/TRIPS

PLAN YOUR ADVENTURE WITH LOCAL EXPERTS

Rough Guides' English-speaking local experts are hand-picked, based on their experience in the travel industry and their impeccable standards of customer service.

SAVE TIME AND GET ACCESS TO LOCAL KNOWLEDGE

When a local expert plans your trip, you save time and money when you book, even during high season. You won't be charged for using a credit card either.

MAKE TRAVEL A BREEZE: BOOK WITH PEACE OF MIND

Enjoy stress-free travel when you use Rough Guides' secure online booking platform. All bookings come with a money-back guarantee.

WHAT DO OTHER TRAVELLERS THINK ABOUT ROUGH GUIDES TRIPS?

Trip to Spain

This Spain tour company did a fantastic job to make our dream trip perfect. We gave them our travel budget, told them where we would like to go, and they did all of the planning. Our drivers and tour guides were always on time and very knowledgable. The hotel accommodations were better than we would have found on our own. Only one time did we end up in a location that we had not intended to be in. We called the 24 hour phone number, and they immediately fixed the situation.

Don A, USA ★★★★★

Trip to Morocco

Our trip was fantastic! Transportation, accommodations, guides – all were well chosen! The hotels were well situated, well appointed and had helpful, friendly staff. All of the guides we had were very knowledgeable, patient, and flexible with our varied interests in the different sites. We particularly enjoyed the side trip to Tangier! Well done! The itinerary you arranged for us allowed maximum coverage of the country with time in each city for seeing the important places.

Sharon, USA ★★★★★

PLAN AND BOOK YOUR TRIP AT
ROUGHGUIDES.COM/TRIPS

CONTENTS

Trip Tips

10 Things not to miss

The high spots of this fascinating and picturesque region cater for all tastes, whether you're a beach fan, bird-spotter, boat enthusiast or culture vulture.

∧ **Boating on the Norfolk Broads.** Hire a boat for the day, take a cruise trip or ideally paddle your own canoe on the delightful waterways of the Norfolk Broads. See page 43.

∧ **Sutton Hoo.** You don't have to be an archaeology buff to enjoy this fascinating site of an Anglo-Saxon burial ship, discovered in 1939. See page 71.

∧ **Ely Cathedral.** Make a detour to this magnificent Norman cathedral that towers above the flat landscape of the Fens. See page 98.

> **Blakeney seals.** Take a boat trip from Morston to Blakeney Point to see a colony of several hundred common and grey seals. See page 38.

∧ **Cambridge.** Hop across the county border to see the fine colleges of this celebrated seat of learning. See page 85.

∧ **BeWILDerwood.** Take the kids to this magical ecofriendly playground with tree houses and zip wires and meet the forest folk who live deep in the woods. See page 45.

∧ **Holkham Hall.** All part of the Holkham estate are the grand Holkham Hall, extensive parklands, nature reserve and the glorious Holkham Bay, with miles of unspoilt golden sands. See page 34.

∨ **Southwold Pier.** This quirky pier is one of the best in the country, and one of the few along the coast to have survived the storms. See page 59.

∨ **Minsmere RSPB Nature Reserve.** Seek out birds and other wildlife at this expertly run reserve, known for bitterns, marsh harriers and avocets. See page 64.

∨ **Norwich Cathedral.** Norwich has many medieval buildings but the magnificent Cathedral, with its soaring spire, is the jewel in the crown. See page 18.

INTRODUCTION TO
Norfolk and Suffolk

Big skies, beaches, boating and birding make Norfolk and Suffolk a haven for outdoor enthusiasts, but they also offer historic churches, fine dining and cosy pubs.

It is hard to believe, when driving through the empty landscapes and sleepy villages of Suffolk and Norfolk, that East Anglia in medieval times was one of the most densely populated and commercialized regions of England.

The broad acres of chalk and grassland provided ideal grazing for sheep, and huge quantities of wool were exported, boosted by the arrival of expert Flemish weavers in the mid-14th century. The main legacy of this era of wealth and prosperity is the region's medieval churches – more than 1,000 of them. It is largely thanks to the region's location, separated from the main north–south axis through Britain, that it has managed to preserve its distinctive architecture, as well as time-honoured traditions and rural character.

Geography

This is the most easterly region of England, bulging out between the shallow Wash to the north

and the River Stour to the south. Characterized by vast skies and hazy, low horizons, the landscape is flat or gently rolling, with shallow valleys and slow-flowing rivers. The region as a whole incorporates some very distinctive areas. The popular Norfolk Broads are a network of navigable rivers and open lakes which were formed by the flooding of shallow pits made by medieval peat diggers. In western Norfolk the sandy heaths of The Brecks were covered in dense woodland until Neolithic man, using axes made from the flint pits at Grimes Graves, cleared the forest for farming. Bordering The Brecks the haunting flat Fenland is one of the richest arable areas of England, but before the 17th century, when the Dutch masterminded the drainage of the fens, this area was marshland, inhabited by fishermen and wildfowlers.

The magnificent coastline provides diverse seascapes, from multicoloured cliffs and golden swathes of sands to wild marshland, tidal creeks and mudflats. Many of the harbours have silted up over the centuries and where

The river by the Pakenham Watermill, Suffolk

A sign in Southwold depicting the Battle of Solebay (1672) between the English and the Dutch

there were once thriving ports there are now coastal villages, with just a handful of fishermen.

When to go

The region has its attractions all year round. It is the driest part of the UK, and ideal for walking or cycling at any time. The warm summer months attract the most visitors, especially to the coast, but even in mid-summer you should be prepared for northerly and easterly winds from the North Sea. May, June, early July and early autumn are good times to go, while the latter part of July and August are invariably the most crowded. Autumn and winter are great times for walking, and especially for birdlife. Thousands of pink-footed geese migrate from Iceland and Greenland, flying inland at dawn to feast on arable farmland. Coasts provide bracing walks off-season, and winter is the best time to see seals on the beach. At the end of the day there is always a cosy pub nearby with local ale and a log fire roaring.

Tourism

Although agriculture and fishing still have a role to play, the economy increasingly relies on tourism. The great outdoors is the main attraction, with walking, touring, visiting beaches and exploring villages the most popular activities. The extensive waterways of the Broads are among the top attractions, both for boating and for rare wildlife. To the east lies exuberant Great Yarmouth, to the north a coast of huge sandy beaches, well-established English seaside resorts such as Cromer and Sheringham, and tiny coastal villages backing on to wildlife-rich creeks and marshes. The Suffolk coast attracts an arty crowd, particularly Aldeburgh with its famous music festival and little Walberswick with its artistic traditions. Inland Suffolk has some idyllic villages, with quaint timber-framed houses, immaculate village greens and vast flint-faced churches.

In addition to great medieval churches, the cultural legacy survives in its Norman keeps, relics of medieval castles, abbeys and monasteries and – from a later era – its magnificent country mansions. Both counties have a vibrant cultural scene with festivals, museums, galleries and arts events. For sightseers the finest towns in the region are Norwich, King's Lynn, Bury St Edmunds and Cambridge (we've crossed over the county border for this unmissable city).

The most notable change in the region in recent years has been the food scene. Pubs, restaurants and cafés have gone from strength to strength, a remarkable number now sourcing high-quality produce from local suppliers. Fashionable delis have taken the place of dusty grocers and Michelin rosettes can be found even on the north Norfolk coast. It's no wonder well-heeled Londoners have been snapping up so many properties here. In desirable spots like Burnham Market or Southwold over half the houses are now second homes.

Coastal environment

For centuries the coastline has faced an ongoing battle with coastal erosion. In the case of Dunwich an entire port was lost to the sea in medieval times. More recently the coast bore the full force of the wild weather in 1953, with the loss of 307 lives in Norfolk, Suffolk, Essex and Lincolnshire. As a consequence storm-surge barriers were constructed on the River Thames and coastal defences were strengthened at high-profile resorts and villages. Others have suffered from more recent tidal surges. Hemsby in Norfolk lost seven houses to the sea in the tidal surge of December 2013. This was the worst storm surge since the 1953 floods, with ferocious waves battering seaside towns and villages and breaching coastal defences. New sea defences at Hemsby were installed in 2015, which held firm in the tidal surge of January 2017. Further schemes have been implemented, but the whole coastal area is constantly under threat. The average loss to the sea is a yard a year, and however great the efforts to protect it, the loss of further coastline is inevitable.

View over Dunwich Heath and the Suffolk coastline

Food and Drink

The last quarter century has seen a transformation of the food and drink scene in Norfolk and Suffolk, thanks to the demand for specialist local producers and the more discerning tastes of holidaymakers.

Thanks to its climate, rich soil and diverse coastline, East Anglia lives up to its reputation as 'the breadbasket of Britain'. Both Norfolk and Suffolk have a field-to-fork philosophy – the idea that food can make its way from the ground to your plate without leaving the county. An encouraging number of gastropubs and restaurants put this philosophy into practice, their menus featuring local fare, whether it's pork from Blythburth, venison from the Suffolk Denholm estate, smoked fish from Orford, crab from Cromer or oysters from Brancaster. Menus often inform you exactly where the produce is sourced. A prime example is *The Bildeston Crown*, Bildeston, whose Red Poll beef, Suffolk lamb and many of the vegetables they serve come from their own farm.

It's not just the food that's home grown. The chances are that your choice of restaurant or pub will be serving real ales and beers from one of the many local micro-breweries. The long-established Adnams in Southwold supplies establishments throughout East Anglia – and well beyond – while Norfolk, which claims to have the best malting barley in the country,

Cromer crab and fish stall in Great Yarmouth

has more micro-breweries than any other county in the UK. To top it off, the Suffolk family-run firm of Aspall have been brewing a range of excellent ciders since 1728.

Many of Suffolk and Norfolk's ancient market towns hold a weekly or monthly farmers' market selling locally made cheeses, artisan bread, ready-to-cook wild game and fresh fish and seafood. Among the best are Snape Maltings, Bury St Edmunds, Lavenham, Sudbury, Swaffam and Creake Abbey.

Fruits of the sea

The fishing scene is not what it was. Lowestoft no longer has a fishing fleet and the silting up of harbours on the North Norfolk coast led to the decline of formerly thriving fishing ports. But crab-catching still goes on in Cromer, mussels are harvested at Brancaster and oysters come from the creeks around Orford. Samphire, otherwise known as 'sea asparagus' thrives in the north Norfolk salt marshes. At Aldeburgh fishermen still land skate, seabass and Dover sole, selling it from shacks on the shingle beach. Stiffkey on the north Norfolk coast is traditionally famous for cockles, known as Stewkey Blues on account of their distinctive grey-blue shells. The cockles are harvested with broad rakes and nets, then steamed or put in soups and pies, although today's cockles are more likely to come from King's Lynn.

The sweet tender Cromer crab is justly famous. These small crustaceans thrive on the chalk reef just off Cromer. No one knows exactly why they're so good (they are the same species as other British crabs) but it is generally thought to be the slow speed with which they grow. Crabbing boats, of which there are now only around a dozen at Cromer, go out to lay pots about three miles offshore from March to October. Try the dressed crab at Davies Fish Shop in Garden Street, Cromer. The legendary Davies family go back four generations as lifeboatmen and fishermen. They have their own boat and you can be assured their seafood is as fresh as you'll get. For a bit of extra excitement, head to Cromer on August Bank Holiday Sunday for the World Crabbing Championships.

Aldeburgh food and drink festival

An increasing number of food festivals are taking place but there is none to match Aldeburgh's, which is a two-day extravaganza in late September in the halls and marquees of Snape Maltings, celebrating the quality and bountiful harvest of the East Suffolk countryside. This is where you can rub shoulders with well-known chefs, meet butchers, bakers and farmers showcasing their produce, attend bread-making sessions, go foraging for nuts and mushrooms or join a tutored wine-tasting session. The event then spreads through the region with farm walks, tastings and workshops across the county for the following fortnight.

Delis and farmshops
SUFFOLK
Emmett's, Peasenhall (www.emmett sham.co.uk). Suffolk hams and bacon made the traditional way since 1820.
Slate Cheese, Aldeburgh (www.slate cheese.co.uk). Award-winning deli.
Suffolk Food Hall, Wherstead, near Ipswich (www.suffolkfoodhall.co.uk). Butcher's, deli, fishmonger, bakery and more all under one roof.
NORFOLK
Farm to Fork & Fish, Horstead (www.farmtoforkandfish.co.uk). Fresh, seasonal and local produce.
The Galley, 43 Lower Street, Horning (www.thegalley-horning.co.uk). Family-run deli, café and gift shop.
Picnic Fayre, Cley-next-the-Sea (www.picnic-fayre.co.uk). Deli with home-made produce, fruit and veg and local products.

Fresh fruit and veg at Picnic Fayre in Cley-next-the-Sea

Market Place and Norwich Castle

TOUR 1

Norwich

Take a step back in time and explore Norwich, an underrated city packed with historical sites and lovely little alleys. This is a full-day 2-mile (3km) walking tour.

Until the Industrial Revolution, Norwich was one of the most prosperous cities in England. Set amid rich agricultural land it rose to prominence in the Middle Ages as a market and trading centre, growing rich on its trade of worsted cloth. Tradition has it that the city had a pub for each day of the year and a church for every Sunday. There were in fact 700 pubs in medieval times, down to around 140 today and declining. Evidence of its former prosperity can be seen in the 32 medieval churches and many historic houses dotted around the city.

Norwich also has a large and colourful market, some great little shops, no shortage of excellent cafés and restaurants and a pleasantly relaxed atmosphere.

Highlights

- Norwich Castle Museum
- Norwich Lanes
- Museum of Norwich
- Elm Hill
- Norwich Cathedral
- Sainsbury Centre for Visual Arts

Norwich Castle

The city's gaunt **Castle** ❶ stands high up on a grassy mound above the city centre. It was built as a royal palace but became the county gaol in 1220 and remained so for 650 years until it was bought by the city for conversion to a museum. The Keep, which is all that remains of the original castle, was refaced in 1834 – hence the newer-than-

Norman look. The battlements and dungeons can be visited on guided tours (additional charge). The Keep has been undergoing a major revamp since 2020, which will see it restored to its former glories by reinstating the Norman floor and recreating Henry I's royal palace. It's set to be completed by 2022.

Castle Museum and Art Gallery

Converted from the old prison blocks, the excellent **Castle Museum and Art Gallery** (tel: 01603 493 625; www.museums.norfolk.gov. uk; July–Sept Mon–Sat 10am–5pm, Sun 1–5pm, Oct–June Mon–Sat 10am–4.30pm, Sun 1–4.30pm) offers a combination of fine art, natural history, archaeology and history. The remarkable array of galleries covers everything from Egyptian and Viking history to the world's largest collection of ceramic teapots. The highlight is the art gallery, with an outstanding collection of paintings by the Norwich School (1803–33), a group of landscape painters who drew their inspiration from the Norfolk scenery. The leading figures were John Crome and John Sell Cotman.

The Royal Arcade

The Royal Arcade

At the castle exit turn right, then right again down the steps, crossing the main road for the **Royal Arcade ❷** a beautiful Art Nouveau thoroughfare.

Market Place

At the end of the arcade you come to the **Market ❸** (Mon–Sat 8am–5pm), which has been held here for over 900 years. It is one of the largest open markets in Britain, with over 190 tightly-packed stalls selling everything from flowers, fresh cockles and

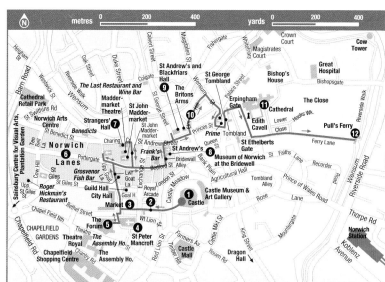

Norwich for kids

There's plenty for children to do in Norwich, starting with the more obvious museums, which also cater for kids' special events, including dressing up. Check the website for Norwich Castle, Bridewell and Strangers' Hall (www.museums. norfolk.gov.uk). The Norwich Puppet Theatre (www.puppettheatre. co.uk) hosts individual and family workshops, activities and events, plus regular shows. For families who enjoy walking, try the self-guided Curious About Norwich walks (www.curiousabout.co.uk), or for the brave hearted, an evening ghost walk (www.ghostwalksnorwich.co.uk) – be prepared for blood and gore and an encounter with the 'Man in Black'.

Cromer crabs to cheap clothes and household goods. Food options are abundant: fish and chips, kebabs, take-away Thai food, mushy peas or stuffed Cromer crabs.

On the far side, looms the massive **City Hall** (1938) with its soaring tower; to the right is the 15th-century **Guildhall**, a fine example of the flintwork for which the city is famous, and to the left, with its tower dominating the city centre, the large perpendicular **Church of St Peter Mancroft** ❹ (Mon–Sat 10am–4pm, winter until 3.30pm, Sun during services only; free). The finest of the city's medieval churches, it has a light and lofty interior with a hammerbeam roof and notable stained glass in the east window depicting the lives of the saints and scenes from the New Testament.

The Forum

In stark contrast to the church is the modern glass-fronted **Forum** ❺ (http://theforumnorwich.co.uk) right opposite, built on the site of the old Norwich Central Library which burnt down in 1995. This horseshoe-shaped building encompasses the regional library, the tourist office, BBC East offices, Fusion (a digital screen gallery), as well as shops and a café. Inevitably controversial when it was built in the heart of the historic city, the Forum has nevertheless become a buzzing centre where people meet or gather in the outdoor plaza to watch amateur performances or free screenings of major sporting events and cinema classics.

Pottergate

Cross the square and take Lower Goat Lane behind the Guild Hall, which takes you down to Pottergate. The alleys here and to the east, across Exchange Street, are known as the **Norwich Lanes** ❻, a lively shopping area with enticing little independent outlets and cafés within lovely old buildings. Turn left at Pottergate and cross into the small square with the flint-faced **Church of St Gregory**,

Alley leading to the Church of St John Maddermarket

Artefacts at the Museum of Norwich at the Bridewell

merchants and mayors of Norwich. There are nooks and crannies to explore and rooms in styles varying from medieval to Victorian.

Retrace your steps to Pottergate, turning left along Lobster Lane, then cross Exchange Street for Bedford Street. Many of the houses here date back to the 17th century.

Museum of Norwich

Turn left into Bridewell Alley for the **Museum of Norwich at the Bridewell** ⑧ (tel: 01603 493 625; www.museums.norfolk.gov.uk; Tues–Sat 10am–4.30pm). The house was a former bridewell, or prison for petty criminals. In the 19th century it became a tobacco factory, later a leather warehouse and finally a shoe factory, making it a fitting setting for a museum devoted to local industries and crafts. Ten galleries chart the history of the city, with plenty of hands-on fun, archive films and recording. Displays show Norwich in its heyday, when it was England's second city. The city's wealth rested on the production and export of elaborate woven fabrics, used for clothing and furnishing. Shoes replaced weaving as the main industry from 1860 and at

which has a medieval wall painting of *St George and the Dragon* in the north aisle. About half of the city's medieval churches are no longer used for regular worship but are beautiful buildings at the heart of the city, and many can still be visited by the public. The Norwich Historic Churches Trust cares for 18 of the churches and most of them have been put to good use. St Gregory's, for example, is leased out as a centre for collectables, with around 30 traders.

Returning to Pottergate, turn left to the flint rubble **Church of St John Maddermarket**, named after the red dye of the madder plant used by the local weavers. A passage under the church tower leads to the Maddermarket Theatre, built in Elizabethan style at the end of the 18th century. The Maddermarket leads up to Charing Cross. Turn left for **Strangers' Hall** ⑦ (tel: 01603 493 625; www.museums.norfolk.gov.uk; June–Sept Wed–Fri 10am–4pm, Sun 1–4.30pm, Oct–May Wed 10am–4pm, Sun 1–4.30pm). This intriguing Tudor house, one of the oldest in Norwich, was once home to wealthy

Getting there

The city of Norwich has direct rail links with London and Cambridge; the station is less than 10 minutes' walk from the centre. If you are coming by car there are five Park and Ride routes to the city centre. Castle Mall is the closest car park to the castle – where the walk begins – but as with all car parks in central Norwich, it's expensive. The VisitNorwich app, available free on iOs and Android, has an interactive map and useful listings.

Retail therapy

Norwich is a great place to shop, whether it's for hand-made Norfolk truffles from Digby's in the Royal Arcade, Cromer crabs from the market, vintage clothes from the Norwich Lanes or fashions or homeware from the award-winning Jarrolds department store. For a treasure trove of Eastern delights check out Country & Eastern (countryandeastern. thesouthasiacollection.co.uk) at 34–36 Bethel Street, next to The Forum. Oriental rugs, kilims, statues and ceramics are laid out in the splendid setting of a former Victorian skating rink.

its peak there were 26 shoe factories employing 26,000 people. On display are elegant examples of footwear, including a thigh-high boot designed for nurses serving in World War II to protect them from snakes and leeches in the Burmese jungle.

St Andrew's to Elm Hill

Follow the alley for **St Andrew's**, a large medieval church with a stained-glass image of Death dancing with a Bishop and fine Renaissance tombs commemorating the Norfolk Suckling family. Cross St Andrew's street for **St Andrew's and Blackfriars Hall** ❾, which together once formed the Dominican Blackfriars convent church. The lofty interior of St Andrew's Hall, whose walls are hung with 127 portraits of former mayors of Norwich, nowadays makes a fine setting for concerts, craft fairs and other events.

Exiting the Hall, turn left up Princes Street and left again for the steeply sloping **Elm Hill** ❿, the city's medieval showpiece. Originally the home of wealthy merchants, the narrow cobbled

street is flanked by beautifully preserved 16th- to 18th-century houses. **The Britons Arms** on the corner is one of the few remaining timber-framed thatched buildings to survive in the city and dates back even further.

Turn right at the end of Elm Hill, up to **Tombland**, the former Saxon market place. To the right, opposite the entrance to the cathedral, lies the quaint Tombland Alley with the 16th-century Steward House on the corner. Take the alley, turning left at the end past the parish Church of St George Tombland. Cross the main street for the cathedral.

Norwich Cathedral

A stunning example of Romanesque architecture, **Norwich Cathedral** ⓫ (tel: 01603 218 300; www.cathedral. org.uk; daily 7.30am–6pm; free but donations welcome; free guided tours Mon–Sat 11am, noon, 1pm, 2pm, 3pm, Sun 1pm, 2pm; evensong Mon–Fri 5.30pm) is a dominant landmark of the city, its 315ft (96-metre) spire the tallest in Britain after Salisbury's. The core of flints and mortar came from East Anglia, but the pale stone of the exterior was shipped all the way from Caen in Normandy. The sheer size and grandeur of the building is

Houses and shopfronts on Elm Hill

The spectacular vaulting and arches inside Norwich Cathedral

best appreciated from the south side (which you'll see on exiting).

To the right of the cathedral entrance is a **memorial to Edith Cavell**, the Norwich-born nurse who was executed by the Germans for helping prisoners of war escape from Belgium during World War I. After the war her body was brought back to Norwich and

buried in the grounds of the Cathedral. The **Erpingham Gate** was built by Sir Thomas Erpingham who led the English archers at Agincourt in 1415 and whose statue occupies a niche over the arch. The gate leads into the tranquil Cathedral Close, where some of the houses originated as monastic buildings. Many of the buildings, including the Church of St Ethelbert, were destroyed in 1272 by rioting citizens.

Cathedral interior

The glorious fan-vaulted roof is supported by mighty Norman pillars and three tiers of arches. The original wooden roof, destroyed by fire, was replaced in the 15th and 16th centuries with stone vaulting and embellished by **carved and painted wooden bosses** illustrating stories from the Bible. There are 1106 of these throughout the cathedral, of which 225 decorate the nave. To see them you will need binoculars, or the mirrors provided.

Beyond the organ screen, the **choir**, where choristers have sung for 900 years, has elaborate wooden carvings on the canopies and also on the misericords (the leaning seats

Spot the peregrines

In 2009 a male peregrine took up residence on Norwich Cathedral spire, and was soon joined by a female. The Hawk and Owl Trust created a nesting platform on the cathedral spire and in spring 2011 the first egg was laid. While the egg failed to hatch, the first successful fledgling was born the following year. The birds have bred each year since then. You can watch the action on a live webcam on the Cathedral website (see page 18) and from a Peregrine Watch Point with telescopes (April–June 10am–4pm, weather permitting).

The Cathedral's soaring spire

Plantation Garden

Adjoining the Catholic Cathedral of St John the Baptist, west of the city centre, the Plantation Garden (www.plantationgarden. co.uk; normally daily 9am–6pm) is one of Norwich's surprises: an idiosyncratic Victorian garden with a 'Gothic' fountain, medieval-style walls, woodland walkways, an Italian terrace and a rustic bridge. Run entirely by volunteers, it is a haven of peace and tranquillity, and a great spot for a picnic.

The Italian terrace and flowerbeds at the Plantation Garden

to support the monks during long services) where medieval scenes, some of them humorous, depict strife, conquest of evil, sloth, greed and mortal sins. Behind the high altar the treasured fragments of the original bishop's throne, placed here by the Normans, lie below the modern wooden throne. Radiating from the ambulatory are small chapels housing medieval painted panels, the finest of which is the highly coloured and detailed *Despenser Retable* (*c.*1380) in St Luke's chapel.

The finely preserved monastic **cloister**, the largest in England, links the cathedral with the modern refectory. Here the roof bosses can be

The Pull's Ferry water gate on the River Wensum

seen more closely and the progression in style of the tracery is evidence of the long period of construction (1297–1430). On the site of the original monks' dining hall is a modern version of a Norman refectory.

The **Lower Close**, where the monastic brew-house and bakehouse used to stand, is today the setting of some very desirable Georgian residences. From here Ferry Lane takes you down to **Pull's Ferry** 🄬, a medieval flint and stone water gate on the River Wensum. This was the route of the medieval canal dug to transport the Caen Cathedral stone on its last leg. From Pull's Ferry there are riverside walks, either north to the medieval **Cow Tower** and beyond, or south, crossing the bridge at the Compleat Angler and continuing on the path on the opposite side of the river.

Sainsbury Centre for Visual Arts

Art lovers should not leave Norwich without a visit to the **Sainsbury Centre for Visual Arts** (tel: 01603 593 199; www.scva.ac.uk; Tues–Fri 9am–6pm, Sat & Sun 10am–5pm; free) at the University of East Anglia (UEA) on the outskirts of the city. Designed by acclaimed architect Norman Foster, it is a hangar-like building created to house Robert and Lisa Sainsbury's wonderful collection of art, featuring works by

Picasso, Henry Moore and Giacometti juxtaposed with ethnographic pieces. Highlights include Moore's *Mother and Child* and an Inca llama effigy, which would probably have been buried as a sacred offering. If you're driving, UEA is well signposted. Alternatively, take bus number 25 from the city centre.

Eating Out

The Assembly House
Theatre Street; tel: 01603 626 402; www.assemblyhousenorwich.co.uk; daily 9am–8.30pm.

The Regency rooms in this historic house make a fine setting for breakfast (9–11.30am), lunch (noon–2pm), dinner (6.30–8.30pm) or, most famously, after-noon tea (noon–4.30pm). A pre-theatre set meal is available before 6.30pm. Sandwiches, scones, cakes and pastries are beautifully presented; mains use locally sourced ingredients. ££

Benedicts
9 St Benedicts Street; tel: 01603 926 080; www.restaurantbenedicts.com; Tues–Sat noon–2pm and 6–10pm.

Chef Richard Bainbridge has a first-class pedigree and has won many accolades, having worked in top-flight restaurants in the UK and beyond. Good-value lunches and excellent a la carte menu, plus a six-course tasting menu, all with wonderful innovative use of East Anglian produce. £££

Frank's Bar
19 Bedford Street; tel: 01603 618 902; www.franksbar.co.uk; Tues–Thurs 9am–midnight, Fri & Sat until 2am, Sun 10am–10.30pm.

A hip little café in the Norwich Lanes serving a great brunch and decent main meals with a Mediterranean twist. Laidback atmosphere, with quirky vintage decor and very late opening hours for Norwich. There's an extensive drinks list, too. £

Grosvenor Fish Bar
28 Lower Goat Lane; tel: 01603 625 855; www.fshshop.com; Mon–Sat 10.45am–7.30pm.

In the Norwich Lanes, this is the city's best chippie, and it's been in the same family for over 30 years. The home-made dips are a fantastic addition, too. The old undercroft downstairs is open for diners to enjoy their meal (eat in or takeaway is the same price). £

The Last Restaurant and Wine Bar
70–6 St George's Street; tel: 01603 626 626; www.lastwinebar.co.uk; Mon–Sat noon–3pm and 6pm–9.30pm.

In a former Victorian shoe factory, this family-run place offers contemporary British cuisine and over 100 wines. The 'Last' refers to the foot-shaped form used to fashion shoes in the days when Norwich was a famous shoe-making centre. ££

Prime
7 Tombland; tel: 01603 765 813; www.primeattheedithcavell.co.uk; Mon–Sat noon–11pm, Sun until 10pm.

Located above the *Edith Cavell* bar, come here for great steak cooked how you like it on hot volcanic stones. It's a carnivore's heaven, but there are fish and vegetarian choices, too. Think gin-cured salmon and mushroom and stilton tagliatelle. ££–£££

Roger Hickman's Restaurant
79 Upper St Giles Street; tel: 01603 633 522; www.rogerhickmans restaurant.com; Wed–Sat noon–2.30pm and 7–10pm.

The set menus at this award-winning restaurant feature delicacies such as foie gras mousse with grapefruit, plum and pickled mushrooms, followed by braised pork cheek and belly with red onion, turnip, chickpea and chorizo stew – and mouthwatering desserts. £££

TOUR 2
The Brecks

Discover the market towns of The Brecks, the wooded paths of Thetford Forest and the stunning ruins of Castle Acre in this one-day, 38-mile (61km) driving tour.

The Brecks is a strange landscape of rolling sandy heaths and large tracts of thick forest. Once covered with heather, grasses, gorse and bracken, many acres are now planted with lofty pine trees, while remaining stretches of heathland are vital habitats for wildlife such as the rare stone curlew and woodlark. The very earliest signs of life can be seen at Grime's Graves, where Neolithic man dug over 400 mines and pits. Thetford Forest is a great spot for outdoor activities, while Thetford and Swaffham, both prosperous trading towns in medieval times, are the main market towns of the area.

Highlights

- Ancient House, Thetford
- High Lodge Thetford Forest
- Grime's Graves
- Oxburgh Hall
- Church of St Peter and St Paul, Swaffham
- Castle Acre Priory

Thetford

In the heart of The Brecks, **Thetford** ❶ was the ancient capital of East Anglia and is traditionally thought to have been the residence of Boudicca, Queen of the Iceni Tribe. At the time of the Domesday Book it was the sixth largest settlement in the country and boasted its own cathedral. The ruins of the great Cluniac Priory can still be explored. The town was also the birthplace of the famous revolutionary philosopher

Thetford Priory

The Peddar's Way

Castle Acre was built at the crossing of the Nar beside the 46-mile (74km) Peddar's Way, the Roman road between central East Anglia and the Norfolk Coast, ending at Holme-next-the-Sea. Now a long-distance footpath, it is well marked and easy going. Castle Acre, with its tempting cafés and pubs, along with accommodation, is a popular stop-off point. For information on the trail see www.nationaltrail.co.uk.

Thomas Paine. On a more frivolous note, Thetford features as Walmington-on-Sea in the hit BBC series *Dad's Army* and now has its very own Dad's Army Museum and a bronze statue of Captain Mainwaring sitting by the river.

Along the central White Hart Street you're unlikely to miss the charming timbered **Ancient House** (tel: 01842 752 599; www.museums.norfolk.gov.uk; April–Sept Tues–Sat 10am–5pm, Oct–March Tues–Sat 10am–4pm), a rare survival from the Tudor period and quite a contrast to Thetford's many newer builds. It is home to the **Museum of Thetford Life**, and includes replicas of the Thetford treasure discovered with a metal detector in 1979 (now in the British Museum), exhibits on flint-knapping and warrening, and a section on Prince Frederick Duleep Singh (1868–1926), last Maharajah of the Punjab, who bequeathed the house to the town in 1921.

Upon leaving the museum, turn right, passing the Church of St Peter, then immediately left for King Street and the **statue of Thomas Paine**. Retrace your footsteps, cross White Hart Street for Minstergate, then walk through the subway to reach **Thetford Priory** (April–Sept 8am–6pm, Oct–

March 8am–4pm; free). After the graffiti-splattered subway these evocative ruins lift the spirit. Founded in the 12th century, the priory was home to treasured relics and became a magnet for pilgrims. Until its suppression by Henry VIII in 1546 this was the burial place of the earls and dukes of Norfolk.

Thetford Forest

For some memorable outdoor adventures, head northwest on the B1107 for Thetford Forest. Turn left when you see signs for **High Lodge Thetford Forest** ❷

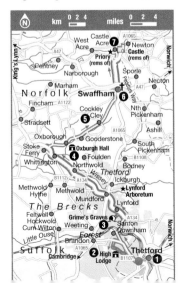

Thomas Paine

Thetford's most celebrated son is Thomas Paine (1737–1809), regarded as one of the greatest radical political writers of the Enlightenment. Paine emigrated to America, where he advocated American independence from Britain in his free-thinking pamphlets, but his greatest work is the *Rights of Man*, in which he espoused the cause of the French Revolution. Paine is commemorated with a statue in front of King's House, Thetford.

The bronze statue of Thomas Paine in front of King's House

(www.forestryengland.uk/high-lodge; daily, check website for closing times; vehicle charge). To explore the forest take a walking trail or cycle path (hire from www.bikearthire.cc), and let the kids loose at WildPlay or Go Ape (tel: 01603 895 500; www.goape.co.uk; prebooking advisable), a great tree-top adventure course with zip wires, tarzan swings and rope ladders. You can even hire a Segway.

Grime's Graves

Exiting the forest turn right and take the first left, a narrow road towards Santon Downham. After the village follow the road north to join the A134. Turn left and you'll soon see a sign for **Grime's Graves** ❸ (tel: 01842 810 656; www.english-heritage.org. uk; April–Sept daily 10am–6pm, Oct Wed–Sun 10am–5pm). This is a 96-acre (39-hectare), lunar-like landscape pitted with over 400 mine shafts. Late Neolithic miners, using antler picks and shovels made from animal shoulder blades, dug deep for the distinctive black flint, hacking through alternating layers of chalk and the paler, less desirable flint to reach the coveted third layer. One shaft is open to the public and visitors can don a

hard hat and descend a 30ft (9-metre) ladder to the bottom of what was a working flint mine. The landscape here is rich in birdlife with skylarks, woodpeckers, nightjars and the very occasional stone curlew.

Rejoin the A134, and unless you want to go straight to Swaffham, cross the roundabout at Mundford, and follow the A134 for **Oxburgh Hall** ❹ (www.nationaltrust.org.uk; daily April–Sept 11am–5pm, Oct 11am–4pm; see website for winter opening times). This

Pew carving in the Church of St Peter and St Paul, Swaffham

The buttercross and statue of Ceres in Swaffham

is an imposing moated mansion, castle-like in its appearance, with a massive Tudor gatehouse. It was built in 1482 by Sir Edmund Bedingfeld and the same family has lived here ever since. In 1950 the 9th baronet was forced to sell and the house was bought by a property developer who intended to demolish the mansion and replace it with 70 houses. But just in the nick of time, three female family members sold their homes and brought the house back to the family. It has been run by the National Trust since 1952. The interior is largely Victorian and features

a priest's hiding hole and needlework hangings executed by Mary Queen of Scots during her captivity.

Swaffham

Continue to Swaffham via **Cockley Cley ❺**, with a pub that boasts the unusual name of *Twenty Churchwardens*. At **Swaffham ❻** the main focus of life is the **Market Cross**, a large square with fine Georgian houses and a **buttercross** (where butter-sellers once displayed their wares), crowned by a statue of Ceres, Roman goddess of grain crops. The square is the scene of a weekly Saturday market and an auction selling bric-à-brac. Off Market Place the **Church of St Peter and St Paul** has a superb double hammerbeam roof, embellished with 192 carved angels. Note too the pews with medieval carvings which include a small man and a dog on a chain. This is the so-called Pedlar of Swaffham. Legend has it that a Thetford man, John Chapman, went to London to seek his fortune and met a man who dreamt he had found treasure under an oak tree in Swaffham. Chapman found the treasure and with the proceeds funded the rebuilding of the church. The Pedlar features on the town sign in Market Cross.

Last but by no means least comes **Castle Acre ❼**, marked off the main road going north from Swaffham. This is a jewel of a village, with rose-clad flint and brick cottages, heralded by the old bailey gatehouse. It is also a rare survival of a Norman-planned settlement, with extensive remains of a castle, priory and massive defences. All three were built by the family of William de Warenne, a veteran of the battle of Hastings. By the late Middle Ages Castle Acre had sunk into relative obscurity, the castle was abandoned and the priory suppressed in 1537. A path off Bailey Street in the village centre

Green Britain

Just off the A47 north of Swaffham lies the Green Britain Centre (www.greenbritaincentre.co.uk; Sept–July Mon–Sat and Aug daily 10am–4pm; guided tours normally at 11am, 1pm and 3pm; visitor centre free, charge for turbine). The wind turbine here has a lofty viewing platform, designed by leading British architect Norman Foster. You have to climb up 300 steps for the view, but it's fairly easy going.

leads to the west gate of the **castle** (free) on a grassy mound in glorious green countryside. The castle is thought to have been built as a combination of fortress and aristocratic residence soon after the Norman Conquest. Wander around the earthworks at this peaceful spot, then head to the far side of the village for **Castle Acre Priory** (tel: 0370 333 1181; www.english-heritage.org. uk; April–Sept daily 10am–6pm, Oct

daily 10am–5pm, Nov–March Sat & Sun 10am–4pm). One of the largest and best preserved monastic sites in the country, it is hugely atmospheric with evocative ruins in a beautiful, tranquil setting. The richly decorated west front, intended to emphasise the prosperity and piety of its founders, is the real show-stopper, but there are other substantial ruins, including the prior's lodging with rooms intact.

Eating Out

THETFORD

Elveden Inn

Brandon Road; tel: 01842 890 876; www.elvedeninn.com; food: Mon–Sat 7.30–9.30am, noon–9pm, Sun 7.30–10am, noon–8pm.

This award-winning pub on the Norfolk/Suffolk border is part of the Guinness-family-owned estate of Elveden, and much of the produce comes from the estate or from other local producers. The full house menu is served all day and there are various Sunday lunch options. Expect local cask ales and of course the best Guinness. ££

OXBOROUGH

Bedingfeld Arms

Opposite Oxburgh Hall; tel: 01366 328 300; www.bedingfeldarms.co.uk; food: Mon–Sat noon–3pm and 6–9pm, Sun noon–8.30pm.

This late 18th-century coach house has well-kept ales, spring lamb and game from the family farm and vegetables and herbs from the kitchen garden. Offerings are a notch up from the average pub: pan-seared duck breast, Norfolk coast moules marinières or venison burger with bacon. ££

COCKLEY CLEY

Twenty Churchwardens

Swaffham Road; tel: 01760 721 439; food: Mon–Sat noon–2pm and 7–9pm, Sun noon–2pm.

This 200-year-old ex-village school serves Adnams Ales and traditional no-frills pub grub, namely home-made pies with veg and gravy (the Churchwarden pie is a favourite). Full of local characters, especially on a Sunday. Cash only. £

SWAFFHAM

CoCoes Café Deli

Strattons Hotel, Ash Close; tel: 01760 723 845; www.strattonshotel.com; Mon–Fri 7.30am–5pm, Sat & Sun 8.30am–5pm.

Set within the grounds of Strattons Hotel, this excellent family-friendly café serves all-day breakfasts, light lunches and a great range of home-made cakes. You can buy local deli products here, too. Dinner and afternoon tea are available at the hotel restaurant (booking required). £

CASTLE ACRE

The Ostrich Inn

Stocks Green; tel: 01760 755 398; www.ostrichcastleacre.com; food: daily noon–3pm, Mon–Sat also 6–9pm.

This inviting coaching inn, which also offers accommodation, has stood on the green for over 400 years. There's a good mix of pub staples and pizzas, plus more exotic choices such as spiced chicken shawarma or grilled lamb kofta. Tasty vegetarian dishes too. ££

Brancaster beach

TOUR 3
King's Lynn to Holkham

A combination of rich heritage, seaside resorts, vast beaches and bird-rich marshes make this 40-mile (64km) tour diverse enough to suit all tastes.

From historic and underrated King's Lynn this route heads north to explore the string of villages along the coast as far as Holkham. Designated as an Area of Outstanding Natural Beauty, the marshes, dunes, sand and shingle provide a haven for birdwatchers, boating enthusiasts and ramblers; while Holkham has one of the most spectacular beaches in the country. To continue from here along the coast to Cromer follow Tour 4 (see page 36). If you want to leave the car at any stage, the Coasthopper bus (see page 122) provides an excellent service from King's Lynn to Cromer, making frequent stops along the way.

King's Lynn

On the Great Ouse, south of the

Highlights

- Tuesday Market Place, King's Lynn
- Sandringham Estate
- RSPB Snettisham Nature Reserve
- Houghton Hall & Gardens
- Titchwell Marsh Nature Reserve
- Holkham Hall

Wash, **King's Lynn ❶** was one of England's major ports from as early as the 12th century, trading with cities of northern Europe. The town was granted various royal charters, the first of them conferred by King John. Following his last visit to the city just before he died in 1216, his royal convoy – carrying all the Crown Jewels – miscalculated the tide and disappeared in The Wash. Or so the story goes. Divers have been searching for the missing treasure ever since.

The sprawling outskirts are unprepossessing but King's Lynn (or 'Lynn' as it's known) has a compact centre with many fine buildings. The town's maritime past is still very much in evidence, with restored Hanseatic warehouses, handsome former merchants' houses and a historic quay on the River Ouse.

Saturday Market Place

The huge twin-towered **King's Lynn Minster** (formerly St Margaret's Church) dominates the market place. On the other side of the square stands the magnificent **Trinity Guildhall** (now the Town Hall; tel: 01553 774 297 (for tours); daily 10am–4pm) with a flint and stone chequerboard facade, stunning 15th-century Stone Hall and splendid Georgian Assembly Room. Beside it is the **Old Gaol House**, which takes you through the more gruesome aspects of the town's history.

Custom House

Take a short walk past the grand buildings and merchants' houses

George Vancouver statue in front of the Custom House, King's Lynn

flanking **Queen Street**. Cobbled alleys from here lead down to the river. The elegant landmark of the **Custom House** on Purfleet Quay, described by the 20th-century art historian Nikolaus Pevsner as 'one of the most perfect buildings ever' has stood here since 1683. It now

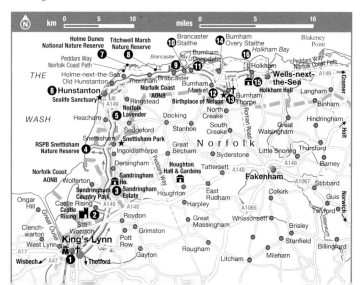

Seahenge

The Lynn Museum (Market Street; www.museums.norfolk.gov.uk; Tues–Sat 10am–5pm, also Sun noon–4pm April–Sept; free Oct–March) has as its centrepiece the remains of a Bronze-Age timber circle. Preserved over the centuries by peat, it was revealed in 1998 during a very low tide at Holme beach. What was assumed to be a ritualistic site was dubbed Seahenge on account of its resemblance to Stonehenge in Wiltshire. After much debate the timbers were removed to the museum for preservation.

serves as the tourist office and a maritime museum where you can find out about Lynn's famous mariners, customs men and smugglers. A statue nearby commemorates George Vancouver, a King's Lynn man who charted 5,000 miles (8,000km) of the west coast of North America in the late 18th century and gave his name to the Canadian city and island.

Tuesday Market Place

Head north along King Street, which is lined by Georgian houses. On the left is the restored early-15th-century **Guildhall of St George**, today home of the King's Lynn Arts Centre. Just beyond it the narrow Ferry Lane leads to the pedestrian ferry which crosses the Ouse to West Lynn. Occupying three acres, the grand and unspoilt **Tuesday Market Place** is one of the finest squares in the country. It is home to the **Corn Exchange** (www.kingslynncornexchange.co.uk) with a pretty neoclassical facade. This now thrives as a multipurpose venue offering a lively programme of concerts, ballet and opera. The town's main market is held in the square, not surprisingly on Tuesdays.

True's Yard Fisherfolk Museum

Turn right at the end of the market, then left for **St Nicholas Chapel** (Tues–Sat 10.30am–4pm; donation welcomed), founded by the Norwich bishops in 1146 and today England's largest surviving parochial chapel.

The chequerboard facade of the Trinity Guildhall, King's Lynn

The Sandringham Estate

Continue along St Ann's Street for **True's Yard Fisherfolk Museum** (tel: 01553 770 479; www.truesyard.co.uk; Tues–Sat 10am–4pm). Dedicated to the local fishing industry, this little museum has two restored fishermen's cottages, a 1904 Lynn fishing smack and the town's last remaining smokehouse. The latter was only discovered a few years ago, having been used as a tattoo parlour and fallen into disrepair. Thanks to a Heritage Lottery Fund the museum bought the premises and restored the smokehouse.

Castle Rising

From King's Lynn follow the A149, signposted Hunstanton. The first left turn beyond the town takes you to **Castle Rising ❷** (Lynn Road; tel: 0370 333 1181; www.castlerising. co.uk; April–Oct daily 10am–6pm, Nov–March Wed–Fri 10am–4pm), one of the largest and finest Norman keeps in the country. It stands at the centre of massive earthworks.

Sandringham

Follow the A149 for another 2 miles (3km) for the **Sandringham Estate ❸** (tel: 01485 545 400; www.sandring

hamestate.co.uk; daily Easter–Sept, except last Wednesday of July, house: 11am–4.45pm, Oct until 4pm; museum: 11am–5pm, Oct until 4pm; gardens: 10.30am–5pm, Oct until 4pm; Country Park free). Bought in 1862 by Queen Victoria for the Prince of Wales (Edward VII to be) and his new wife, Princess Alexandra, the estate passed down through four generations of monarchs and is now the country retreat of the Queen. The

Relaxing at Norfolk Lavender

house is surrounded by the 600-acre (243-hectare) **Country Park**. There is no charge to the public and many visitors come for picnics, cycle rides and nature trails through the woodland or for the shops, restaurant or café at the well-organized Visitor Centre. Visitors can also see the beautiful medieval **Church of St Mary Magdalene**, where the Royal Family worship while they are at Sandringham. The main ground floor rooms of the house, used by the royal family, are open to the public, as is the museum housing royal memorabilia, and 60 acres (24 hectares) of glorious gardens.

Norfolk Lavender

The A149 continues north to **Snettisham**, home to the **RSPB Snettisham Nature Reserve** ❹, well known for the spectacular winter flights of waders and wildfowl flying in from The Wash, just before high tide. From Snettisham northwards the A149 can become traffic clogged in summer, with crowds heading for the beaches. At Heacham, **Norfolk Lavender** ❺ (tel: 01485 570 384; www.norfolk-lavender.co.uk; April–Oct 9am–5pm,

---

Snettisham Park

Close to Snettisham Church and signposted from the A149, Snettisham Park (tel: 01485 542 425; www.snettishampark.co.uk; daily 10am–4pm, check online for Nov–Jan) is a working farm where children can bottle feed orphan lambs, feed the goats and collect eggs from the hens. Fun rides on tractors take you close up to a herd of red deer with over 60 hinds and two stags. For countryside trails pick up maps from the Visitor Centre.

Nov–March 9am–4pm; free) brings in coachloads of tourists, not just for the summer blaze of colour from the lavender, but for the large gift shop, selling all manner of lavender products, the Walsingham Farm Shop, with delicious local pies and cheeses (a good spot to pick up a picnic) and the tea room. Children's attractions are the collection of rare farm breeds, the outdoor play area and Farmer Fred's Adventure Play Barn, an indoor soft play centre.

Houghton Hall & Gardens

One of Britain's finest Palladian houses, Houghton Hall (www.houghtonhall.com) was built in the 1720s by Britain's first Prime Minister, Sir Robert Walpole. Restored to its former glory by the Marquess of Cholmondeley, the hall remains much as it was in Walpole's day, though the collection of Old Masters was sold to Catherine the Great and are in the Hermitage in St Petersburg, Russia. The outstanding grounds feature an award-winning 5-acre (2-hectare) walled garden and a deer park.

Houghton Hall

Hunstanton beach is great for families

Hunstanton

Two miles (3km) north of Heacham, **Hunstanton** ❻ (or 'Hunston' as the locals call it) is the only East Anglian resort facing west, and as such enjoys some glorious sunsets over the Wash. It was here that St Edmund, King of East Anglia, is said to have landed in AD 850, the ruins of St Edmund's Chapel marking the spot. Today it is a popular family seaside resort, with a fine, gently-sloping sandy beach, and cliffs behind which are distinctive for their coloured stripes of carrstone

and red and white chalk. Quiet old Hunstanton to the north is very different from the centre, where the beach with pony rides is backed by a promenade of seaside amusements, a bingo hall and a Sealife Sanctuary (www.visitsealife.com). The sandy beach is 2 miles (3km) long and good for exploring rock pools, collecting shells or enjoying the shallow waters of the sea (though it's a long walk to the water at low tide). Searles Sea Tours (tel: 01485 534 444; www.seatours. co.uk) organize coastal trips and one-hour seal safaris. Trips depend on the tides so it's best to ring in advance.

Nelson's Norfolk

The great naval hero pops up everywhere in this part of Norfolk, and it's hardly surprising. He was born at Burnham Thorpe, learnt to sail at Burnham Overy Staithe and drank at the local pubs. You'll also find Nelson memorabilia in Burnham Thorpe Church. Great Yarmouth on the east coast has the only museum dedicated to Nelson (see page 50) and the soaring Nelson Monument, in what is these days a rather grim area of the town.

Holme Dunes and Titchwell Marsh Nature Reserves

The A149 follows the coast eastwards through a series of small villages. **Holme-next-the-Sea** is the end (or start) of the **Peddar's Way**, crossing here with the **Norfolk Coast Path**, which runs all the way from here to Sea Palling (63 miles/101km). The sand dunes, marshes and reed beds attract waders and migrant wildfowl, as well as nesting birds such as oystercatchers and ringed plover in spring and summer. The **Holme Dunes National Nature Reserve** ❼ is one of a series of connecting nature reserves along this coast. But the key one is **Titchwell Marsh Nature Reserve** ❽ (tel: 01485 210 779; www.rspb.org.uk; daily dawn to dusk; car park charge for non-members) beyond Thornwell. Dubbed 'Twitchwell', it is a mix of marsh, reedbed and beach, which bring thousands of migrating birds and a wide variety of species throughout the year including marsh harriers, avocets, bearded tits and bitterns.

Brancaster

Next along the A149 is **Brancaster** ❾ which has a wonderfully unspoilt beach, backed by the renowned Royal West Norfolk Golf Club. The village merges into **Brancaster Staithe** ❿, popular for sailing and fishing. Brancaster is famous for mussels and you can find them for sale, along with lobster, crabs, whelks and cockles, at the Crab Hut at the Staithe or dished up at *The White Horse* restaurant (see page 35). The favourite local watering hole is *The Jolly Sailors*

Burnham Market sign

pub with its own Brancaster Brewery ale, a popular spot for thirsty walkers from the Norfolk Coast path, 150yds/metres away.

The Burnham Villages

Between Brancaster and Holkham there are seven Burnham villages, three of them now merging as Burnham Market. Brancaster merges into **Burnham Deepdale** ⓫, which has a church with a round Saxon tower and a Norman font with carved panels of farming scenes depicting each month of the year (press the button by the curtain to light them up). **Burnham Market** ⓬, signed off to the right just after Burnham Norton, is the showpiece village, popularly known as Chelsea-on-Sea. It has a wide green of handsome Georgian houses, lovely little shops, galleries and top-notch delis. Many of the houses here are second homes; those without their own can stay at the delightful *Hoste* (see page 125), a hub of the village.

Take the Fakenham Road from Burnham Market and at the first turn left for **Burnham Thorpe** ⓭, famous as Nelson's birthplace (see page 32). His house disappeared long ago but you can see a plaque where it stood, in the south of the village. The 13th-century **All Saints' Church**, where Nelson's father was rector, is full of Nelson memorabilia, including the cross and lectern that were constructed from *HMS Victory* timbers. England's great Admiral may well have taken his first sailing lesson at **Burnham Overy Staithe** ⓮ before he went to sea at the age of 12. The village was established when the River Burn silted up and boats could no longer reach the seaport, at what is now Burnham Overy Town. It is still a sailing centre, and the harbour in the creek is the starting point for seasonal ferry trips

Horseriding along Holkham Bay

(two hours either side of high tide) to the nature reserve of Scolt Head.

Holkham

Last on the route is **Holkham**, a remarkable combination of history, architecture, wildlife and sweeping coastal landscape. It is all part of the estate of **Holkham Hall** ⑮ (tel: 01328 713 111; www.holkham.co.uk; hall: April–Oct Sun, Mon & Thurs noon–4pm; museum, walled gardens, play area, café and shop: daily 10am–5pm; park daily 9am–5pm).

Set within magnificent rolling parkland, the sombre Palladian facade belies a grandiose hall and state rooms with, among others, paintings by Van Dyck, Gainsborough and Rubens. The house was built for Thomas Coke, first Earl of Leicester, in the 18th century and is occupied by his descendant, Edward Coke. The remarkable number of attractions includes a yearly themed exhibition, the extensive grounds with 18th-century walled gardens, the deer park and lake where you can hire a canoe, kayak, rowing boat or try your hand at water zorbing. Cycles can be hired to explore the estate's extensive grounds.

Holkham Bay

Access to **Holkham Bay** ⑯ is via the salt marshes, along Lady Anne's Drive opposite Holkham Hall and on a sunny day packed with parked cars (the beach can also be reached from the next resort, Wells-next-the-Sea, see page 36). Follow the boardwalk through pinewoods to reach what is one of the most spectacular beaches of East Anglia: a huge swathe of sands where even in peak season you can find a peaceful stretch. Low tide reveals miles of beach, and in summer a mass of purple sea lavender.

Purple sea lavender

Eating Out

KING'S LYNN
Mem's Kitchen

69 High Street; tel: 01553 777 624; memskitchen.co.uk; Mon, Wed–Sat 9am–3pm, Sun 10am–3pm.

Mem's Kitchen is all about fresh Mediterranean food. They have a lengthy menu ranging from crowd pleasers such as falafel to mix meze. All their cakes are home-made, opt for the chocolate Nutella cake if you have an especially sweet tooth. It's a great spot for a light lunch too, with plenty of healthy salads. ££

SNETTISHAM
Rose and Crown

Old Church Road; tel: 01485 541 382; www.roseandcrownsnettisham.co.uk; all-day menu noon–9pm, Sun until 8.30pm.

Everything you would hope from an English village pub: an ancient rose-clad inn with low ceilings and old beams, log fires, great food and ales and a warm welcome. Seafood and samphire come from Brancaster, asparagus and strawberries from local farmers and game 'from the gentlemen in wellies in the back bar'! ££

RINGSTEAD
The Gin Trap Inn

6 High Street; tel: 01485 525 264; www.thegintrapinn.co.uk; food: Mon–Thurs noon–2pm and 6–8.30pm, Fri & Sat noon–2.30pm and 6–9pm, Sun noon–4pm and 6–8pm.

Although named after the traps for catching game, rather than the alcoholic spirit, the new owners have taken the opportunity to present some 120 gins to the clientele. The varied menu highlights local produce and will appeal to meat and fish eaters, as well as catering for vegetarians. Ringstead is a picturesque village on the Peddars Way footpath. £–££

THORNHAM
Shucks

Thornham Road; tel: 01485 525 889; Mon–Fri 10am–9pm, Sat 9.30am–9pm, Sun 9.30am–6pm.

This is one to tick off the bucket list – having a meal in a yurt. Phil and Beth Milner are keen to deliver 'honest, rustic food' using produce from the Drove Orchards kitchen gardens where the yurt is based. Service can at times be rather tardy, so expect the possibility of a delay. ££

BRANCASTER STAITHE
The White Horse

Main Road; tel: 01485 210 262; www.whitehorsebrancaster.co.uk; daily noon–2pm and 6.30–9pm, bar menu throughout the day.

Enjoy spectacular views over the tidal marsh from the conservatory restaurant. This is definitely a place to try simply-cooked local fish and seafood. Samphire comes from the salt marsh and mussels and oysters are farmed and harvested at the bottom of the garden. ££

BURNHAM MARKET
Number 29 Bar & Restaurant

29 Market Place; tel: 01328 738 498; www.number-29.com; Mon–Sat 8.30am–11pm, Sun 8.30am–10pm.

This classy restaurant is the flashiest culinary experience in the area. The decor is grand with black and white photographs plastered over the walls and cosy fireplaces to settle around. It serves breakfast and lunch, but dinner is something really special with loin of deer and ribeye steak on the menu. All the restaurant's meat is sourced locally. ££

Seal-spotting trip to Blakeney Point

TOUR 4
Wells to Cromer

This 30-mile (48km) day tour takes in some of the very best of Norfolk: dramatic seascapes, quaint coastal villages, seal-spotting at Blakeney and delicious crabs at Cromer.

This route takes you from Wells-next-the-Sea to Cromer, taking in wide stretches of beach, marsh and mud flats, pebble shores and seaside resorts. At low tide the sea almost disappears into the distance leaving a wealth of seashells and shallow pools for children to play in. Inland the landscape is gently rolling with pretty villages, flint cottages and plenty of welcoming pubs. Be aware that the A149 is very narrow in parts and villages like Cley-next-the-Sea can become traffic-clogged in high season. The western stretch of the north Norfolk coast is covered in Tour 3 (see page 27).

Wells-next-the-Sea

Before the silting up of the harbour, **Wells-next-the-Sea** ❶ really did sit

Highlights

- Wells-next-the-Sea
- Seal trips from Morston
- Blakeney
- Cley Marshes Nature Reserve
- Sheringham Park
- Felbrigg Hall
- Cromer Pier

next to the sea. It was a major port of East Anglia and whelks were its main industry. Although a shadow of its former self, it is still a working port. Fishing boats bring in crabs, lobsters and whelks, and coasters still anchor along the quayside. The Dutch North Sea clipper, *Albatros*, dating from 1899, is a permanent feature here,

Colourful beach hut, Wells-next-the-Sea

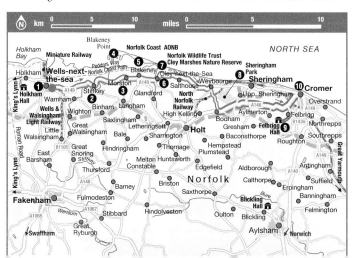

Retail treats

Cley-next-the-Sea's High Street boasts a fine selection of little shops: the family-run Cley Smokehouse (www.cleysmokehouse.com) where everything is smoked on site, the neighbouring Made In Cley (www.madeincley.co.uk) with tempting pieces of pottery made on the premises, the Pink Foot Gallery (www.pinkfootgallery.co.uk) devoted to contemporary nature-inspired art and Picnic Fayre (www.picnic-fayre.co.uk), an award-winning deli in an historic old forge. Inland, Holt has some fine art galleries, two excellent bookshops, several stylish clothes boutiques, plus Bakers and Larners (www.bakersandlarners.co.uk), described by some as 'the Fortnum & Mason of East Anglia'.

offering real ales and Dutch specialities above and below deck, live music at weekends (ranging from punk to Irish folk) and even bed and breakfast (www.albatroswells.co.uk). The resort has a lively centre with small shops, abundant cafés, chippies and stalls selling seafood. It also has a lovely leafy Georgian square, called the Buttlands, with two former coaching inns, both offering attractive accommodation and fine dining.

The beach

The vast and dramatic sandy beach, backed by pine-clad dunes, is a mile from the centre, and can be accessed either by foot along **The Bank** or on the narrow-gauge harbour railway. At low tide it's over a mile down to the water's edge, but when the tide turns it comes in fast and can catch tourists

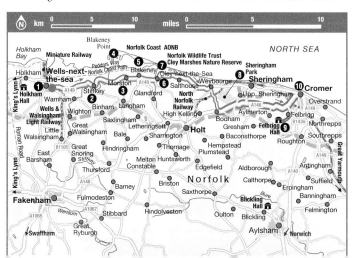

Paddling at Blakeney Point

unaware. This is probably Norfolk's best surveyed beach, equipped with a volunteer coastwatch (www.coastwatch wells.org.uk) and official lifeguards, on duty from early July until early September (10am–6pm).

Stiffkey

The A149 passes right through the little village of **Stiffkey ❷**, traditionally famous for 'Stewkey blues', or cockles, collected from the salt marshes to the north of the village and coloured blue from the mud. Today, however, any cockles you find on menus or at seafood stalls will have come from King's Lynn. The **Rescue Wooden Boats** charitable trust (www.rescue woodenboats.com) is working to restore and re-use crab and whelk boats and other heritage working craft. Their Maritime Heritage Centre (April–Oct Sat & Sun 11am–3pm) is signed to the left off the main road.

Blakeney

Next along is **Morston ❸**, where ferries depart from the quay for seal-spotting trips to **Blakeney Point ❹** (tel: 01263 740 241; www.bishops boats.com; mid-March–Oct daily according to tides; advance booking

advisable). Blakeney Point is home to a colony of common and grey seals, which bask on the sands when the tide is low. Trips last roughly an hour but when tides and conditions allow, boats can also stop on Blakeney Point Nature Reserve, adding between 30 minutes and 1 hour to the trip. The tip of Blakeney Point is the summer home of about a dozen species of seabirds, including a large colony of terns.

Blakeney ❺ itself, a little further on, is a lovely little coastal village of flint-cobbled cottages, with a fine church and a tiny harbour with small yachts and footpaths along mudflats and salt marshes. Birdwatchers flock here all year round and it's very popular for sailing. Like so many of the coastal villages, Blakeney was a major harbour before the silting up of the estuary. Now only small boats can navigate the waters.

Cley-next-the-Sea

East of Blakeney, **Cley-next-the Sea ❻** (pronounced 'Cly') became the first Wildlife Trust Nature Reserve in 1926. The combination of salt marshes, reed beds and lagoons attract a remarkable amount of birdlife, both breeding and migratory. Details of local sightings are

The Poppy Line

The resort of Sheringham was a small fishing village before the North Norfolk Railway was established in 1887. It was axed 77 years later by Dr Beeching, but local enthusiasts were determined to preserve Norfolk's most scenic stretch of railway, with steam services starting in 1976. The scenic Poppy Line of The North Norfolk Steam Railway (www.nnrailway.co.uk), operated largely by volunteers, carries over 165,000 passengers a year and chugs five miles (8km) between Sheringham and the lovely little Georgian town of Holt.

Conductor on The North Norfolk Steam Railway

on display at the excellent ecofriendly Visitor Centre (daily 10am–5pm, until 4pm in winter; free) of the **Norfolk Wildlife Trust Cley Marshes Nature Reserve ❼** beyond the village on the right. Lazy birders can sit in the panoramic café with its wonderful coastal views, spotting birds using the telescopes provided. Serious ones will spend the day in the reeds and marshes, or in the hides that provide fine views over saline pools and scrapes. There is good birding all year round, whether it's spotted redshank in spring, avocet or spoonbills in summer, waders in

Cley Windmill

August and September or wildfowl in winter. Birds apart, Cley is a delightful village of flint and brick cottages and enticing little shops (see page 37). A prominent landmark is the 18th-century **Cley Windmill**, which has been converted into a very appealing guesthouse (see page 125). The architectural highlight of the village is the **Church of St Margaret** on the Holt Road, a glorious medieval church with a soaring tower, beautifully carved porch and fine carvings inside. Sadly the work on the church in the 14th century was never completed: the Black Death in 1349 killed half the population of Cley and work came to a standstill.

Sheringham Park

Continue along the A149 through Salthouse to Weybourne, turning right opposite the church, then immediately left, following signs to Bodham. When you reach the A148 turn left. In about 1.5 miles (2km) you will see a sign for **Sheringham Park ❽** (tel: 01263 820 550; www.nationaltrust.org.uk; daily dawn to dusk; free but parking charge for non-members), designed in 1812 by landscape gardener Humphry Repton.

The walled garden at Felbrigg Hall

This splendid 1,000-acre (405-hectare) park has landscaped and woodland gardens with some stunning coastal views, particularly from the Gazebo, a tower at treetop height. The park can be explored on waymarked trails.

Felbrigg Hall

Continue on the A148 for about 4 miles (6km), turning right on to the B1436, signed **Felbrigg Hall ❾** (tel: 01263 837 444; www.nationaltrust.org.uk; early March–Oct Sat–Tues 11am–5pm, daily during school holidays), a wonderful Jacobean mansion filled with 18th-century furnishings and paintings collected on the Grand Tour. No less impressive is the extensive parkland, with woodland and lakeside paths and a lovely walled garden with espalier fruit trees, abundant flowering plants and an 18th-century octagonal dovecote.

Cromer

The final stop is **Cromer ❿**, dramatically poised on a high bluff. This pleasantly old-fashioned seaside resort became popular with the advent of the railway. Behind the long sand and shingle beach the town centre is dominated by its parish church whose soaring tower, with 172 steps, is the tallest in Norfolk. Cromer is best known for its pier, whose Pavilion Theatre still packs in audiences, and for the famous Cromer crab, sold throughout Norfolk from Easter to October. You won't have to go far in town before finding a stall or restaurant offering Cromer dressed crab.

Cromer Pier

The splendid Cromer Pier lies below the Victorian *Hôtel de Paris*, whose guest list includes the Prince of Wales (the future Edward VII) and Oscar Wilde, who stayed here in 1892.

Cromer Pier

One of the few surviving piers along the East Anglian coastline, it has a restaurant, gift shop, a life boat station and the only 'End of the Pier Show' in Europe. Cromer's **Pavilion Theatre** (www.cromerpier.co.uk) has been producing a live variety show since 1977. Shows take place from Easter to September and are full of glitz and glamour, with West End and Broadway-style song and dance numbers. Celebrities appear from time to time.

A tidal surge in December 2013 nearly put a stop to the show. This wouldn't have been the first disaster. The wooden jetty built in 1822 was swept away in a storm, the replacement washed away before the paint was barely dry, the third lasted until 1897 when it was torpedoed amidships by a coal boat during a storm. Today's pleasure pier dates from 1901. Despite an attempt to blow it up in World War II to prevent it being used as a landing stage by invading forces, damage wrought by the 1953 and 2013 tidal surges and a bulk barge slicing through it in 1993, it is still here today – a testament to Victorian engineering.

Seafront supper, Cromer

Cromer museums and zoo

At the end of the promenade the **Henry Blogg Museum** (tel: 01263 511 294; www.rnli.org.uk; April–Sept Tues–Sun 10am–5pm, Oct–March until 4pm; free) is named after Cromer's celebrated coxwain (1876–1954) who served for 53 years, saved 873 lives and became a national hero. The centrepiece is Blogg's life boat, *H.F. Bailey*. Inland, next to Cromer Church, the **Cromer Museum** (tel: 01263 513 543; www.museums.norfolk.gov. uk; Mon–Fri 10am–4pm, Sat & Sun noon–4pm) gives you an insight into Cromer when it was a Victorian seaside

Blickling Hall

Ten miles (16km) south of Cromer, Blickling Hall (www.nationaltrust.org. uk; daily noon–5pm; weekends only in winter noon–4pm; park free) creates quite an impact: a magnificent red-brick Jacobean mansion crowned by turrets, chimneys and gables. The interior gives you an insight into both upstairs and downstairs life in the Edwardian era but the extensive grounds are the main attraction with a lake amidst the park and woodland. There are several miles of footpaths and bridle paths and cycles can be hired.

Exploring the gardens at Blickling Hall

resort with fine hotels. South of the town the **Amazona Zoo** (Hall Road; tel: 01263 510 741; www.amazona zoo.co.uk; daily mid-March–Oct 10am–5pm, Nov & Dec & mid-Feb–

mid-March 10am–3.30pm) has animal species from tropical South America in a wooded setting. The zoo works with conservationists and the animals are not taken from the wild.

Eating Out

WELLS-NEXT-THE-SEA
The Crown Hotel
The Buttlands; tel: 01328 710 209; www.crownhotelnorfolk.co.uk; Mon–Sat noon–2.30pm and 6.30–9pm, Sun noon–9pm.

Part of The Flying Kiwi Inns group, owned by New Zealand-born celebrity chef Chris Coubrough, this boutique hotel offers fine dining in the restaurant's spacious orangery. Afternoon teas are on offer too – with or without Prosecco. ££

BLAKENEY
Blakeney Hotel
The Quay; tel: 01263 740 797; www.blakeney-hotel.co.uk; daily noon–2pm and 6.30–9pm, Sat until 9.30pm.

One of the coast's loveliest hotels, the Blakeney serves first-class food with fine views across the estuary. Non-residents are welcome at breakfast, lunch or dinner. Come for Blakeney fish soup, home-made burgers, whole dressed local crab, fillet of sea bass or roast Norfolk fillet of beef. £££

MORSTON
Morston Hall
A149 between Blakeney and Stiffkey; tel: 01263 741 041; www.morstonhall. com; dinner daily at 7.15pm, lunch Sun at 12.15pm.

Luxury dining in a smart country-house hotel. Michelin-starred chef Galton Blackiston features local produce such as Blakeney lobster and Morston mussels on the menu. The dinner tasting menu of seven courses changes daily. Reservations essential. £££

CROMER
No 1 Cromer
1 New Street; tel: 01263 515 983; www.no1cromer.com; downstairs: daily noon–8pm, closes 7pm Sun; upstairs: Wed–Fri noon–3pm and 5.30–9pm, Sat noon–8.30pm, Sun noon–7pm; Ice Cromer: 11am–8pm.

Upmarket chippie opened by Galton Blackiston of *Morston Hall* (see opposite) and an upstairs restaurant with great sea, pier and sunset views. The short menu may feature Cromer crab burger, seafood paella and barbeque chicken supreme. End with a hot sugar donut or ice cream at Ice Cromer on the corner of New Street. ££

The Old Rock Shop Bistro
10 Hamilton Road; tel: 01263 511 926; www.oldrockshopbistro.co.uk; daily 8am–6pm.

Popular bistro billed as serving light breakfasts, tasty lunches and hearty dinners. Choose from Cromer crab specials or Thai fishcakes, freshly baked pastries to sticky barbeque ribs. £

HOLT
The Folly Tearoom
4 Hoppers Yard, Bull Street; tel: 01263 713 569; www.follytearoom.co.uk; Mon–Sat 9am–6pm, also July & Aug Sun 10am–4pm.

Perfectly hidden away and with a delightful garden for summer eating, this is the quintessential English tearoom. All the 'Folly' menus are mouth-watering, from the 'Full Folly Breakfast' to 'Folly Traditional' afternoon tea. Light lunches available too. £

Canoeing on Wroxham Broad

TOUR 5

Norfolk Broads

This whole-day 34-mile (55km) driving tour, with optional walks and boat trips, explores the timeless landscape of the Norfolk Broads, the largest protected wetland in the UK.

Norfolk's main tourist draw, the Broads, are an extensive network of navigable rivers and lakes, fens, marshes and wet woodlands. The shallow lakes, or broads, were created by the gradual flooding of shallow pits that had been created by medieval peat-diggers. Today the waterways are a haven for boating holidaymakers, walkers, cyclists and wildlife enthusiasts. Although much of the plant and animal life has disappeared, many of the broads are now nature reserves. Remember to wear sturdy shoes or wellies – this is a wetland, even in summer. If time allows, take one of the small boat trips from various spots across the Broads – there's nothing like seeing them from the water.

Highlights

- Ranworth Broad Wildlife Centre
- Church of St Helen, Ranworth
- BeWILDerwood
- Hickling Broad
- Horsey Windpump and seals at Horsey

Ranworth Broad

Start your tour 4 miles (6km) east of Wroxham at the village of **Ranworth**, peacefully set on the Malthouse Broad in the valley of the River Thurne. Norfolk Wildlife Trust runs boat trips from here to the superb floating **Ranworth Broad Wildlife Centre ❶** (free) where visitors can take another boat for a tour around the broad.

Alternatively, take the 10–15 minute walk along the leafy boardwalk via reed and sedge beds with rare aquatic plants. Look out for rare butterflies, dragonflies and damsel flies as you go. The glass-panelled wildlife centre has wonderful views of wildfowl on the water. This is a family-friendly spot with chatty staff and plenty of nature activities for children. Carefully positioned webcams focus on the antics of the wildfowl on the water. There are always birds to see, especially terns diving for fish.

Back at Ranworth don't miss the **Church of St Helen ❷** above the village. Known as 'the Cathedral of the Broads', this has a beautifully decorated medieval roodscreen portraying the apostles and popular saints of the period, a rare illuminated antiphoner (service book) and – for the energetic – glorious views from the top of the bell tower (89 steep steps up).

Salhouse Broad and Hoveton Great Broad

Drive from Ranworth to Salhouse via the pretty village of **Woodbastwick ❸** with its thatched houses. Before the village of Salhouse you'll see a wooden sign for **Salhouse Broad ❹** (tel:

The view from the Church of St Helen, Ranworth

01603 722 775; www.salhousebroad. org.uk), a broad of around 40 acres (16 hectares) reached by a 10-minute woodland walk. This is a popular spot for canoe hire, as well as ferry trips (Easter–Sept Fri–Sun 10am–3pm) to the nature trail on **Hoveton Great Broad ❺**, another haven for wildlife.

Wroxham

Drive on to Salhouse, turning right for **Wroxham ❻**. Be forewarned that this small town's centre is notorious for traffic jams, especially at weekends. The so-called 'Capital of the Norfolk

Wroxham Barns

North of Wroxham on the Tunstead Road, the Wroxham Barns complex (www.wroxhambarns.co.uk; daily 10am–5pm) is a favourite with youngsters, particularly for its Junior Farm where children can watch pigs being fed, groom the ponies, collect eggs from the henhouse and bottle feed spring lambs. The site includes craft studios, clothes boutiques, children's funfair and a mini-golf course. There is also an excellent restaurant (see page 49).

Children will love the Junior Farm at Wroxham Barns

appear to own half the village, and have what's universally known as 'the world's biggest village store'. Stock up in their Food Hall for a picnic or head straight on, taking the main right turn after the bridge signposted Potter Heigham, A1062.

BeWILDerwood

Just before Horning you'll see signs for **BeWILDerwood** ❼ (tel: 01692 633 033; www.bewilderwood.co.uk; Feb half term until end of Oct half term, 10am–5.30pm, but check website before visiting). If you have children in tow, particularly 2–12-year-olds, this is not to be missed. There's oodles of fun here. Extending over 50 acres of woodland and marshland, it is a magical playground of tree houses,

Broads', it is a boaties' paradise, equipped with every nautical need. The famous Roys of Wroxham, in the same family since the 19th century,

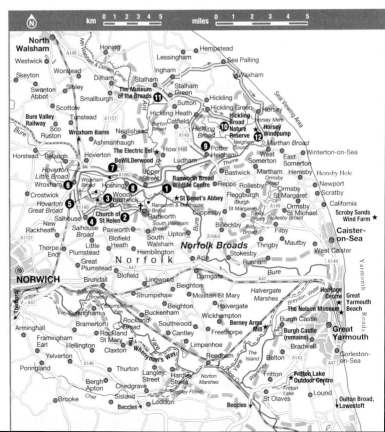

Spot the seals

Horsey is only about a mile from the sea and the beach between here and Winterton-on-Sea is home to a colony of seals that come to breed. Turn left before you reach the Windpump, along a track marked 'seal viewing area'. From here it's a 20-minute walk – and well worth it as you can often see seals bobbing up and down in the waves. In winter you can see large numbers of them offshore.

A couple of friendly seals near Horsey

aerial ropewalks and wobbly zip wires, reached by boat or boardwalk. The whole site is built from sustainable wood. Creator and owner Tom Blofeld drew on happy childhood memories (he grew up here) to create the adventure playground and the magical forest folk who live deep in the woods, among them Swampy, a young Marsh Boggle, the lugubrious Thornyclod Spider and the goblin-like Twiggles. The characters feature in Tom's wonderful book *A Boggle at BeWILDerwood* which, with his other books (and audio book), are on sale at the site.

Horning

Take the next right turn for the pretty riverside village of **Horning ⑧**. If you're in need of sustenance there is plenty of choice here: *The Swan Inn* has a lovely setting by the waterside, *The New Inn* serves good food and a great pint and the *Bure River Cottage Restaurant* is a fabulous seafood spot (see page 49, dinner only). A plaque in the centre of Horning shows the path from the village along the River Bure to **St Benet's Abbey**. The evocative 12th-century ruin, standing in isolation, was originally on an island and has become an iconic symbol of the Broads. This is still a place of

worship and the Bishop of Norwich takes an annual service here on the first Sunday of August.

Hickling Broad

Continue east along the A1062 through the quiet village of Ludham for **Potter Heigham ⑨**, a boating centre best known for its low-arched medieval bridge where many an amateur sailor has floundered. There is little to detain you in the village so turn left on to the A149, signed Stalham. Take the first right turn, marked Hickling, and follow signs to the village, which bring you to *The Greyhound Inn*, an excellent place for a

Tree houses at BeWILDerwood

Pleasure boating on Horning Broads

pit stop (see page 49). Turn right at the pub, following signs for the Nature Reserve and Visitor Centre.

Set in the upper stretches of the River Thurne, **Hickling Broad** (www.norfolkwildlifetrust.org.uk/hickling) is the largest of the Norfolk Broads. With its wide skies and open landscape it's a lovely spot for a walk. Various trails start from the **Nature Reserve ❿**. Keep an eye out for swallowtail butterflies, bitterns, cranes, lapwings, marsh harriers and other birds and insects. The Water Trail takes you by electric-powered boat across open water to the 60ft (18-metre) tree tower with its views of the broad. It's worth hiring binoculars from the Visitor Centre (deposit required), and booking is recommended for boat trips (tel: 01692 598 276).

The Museum of the Broads

Return to *The Greyhound Inn*, turn right and take the second left towards Stalham. After just over 2 miles (3km) turn left and immediately right for the A149, then head towards Stalham. You'll see the **The Museum of the Broads ⓫** (The Poor's Staithe; tel: 01692 581 681; www.museumofthebroads.org.uk; July–Oct Sun–Fri 10am–4.30pm, Sat 10am–10pm, closed Fri in Oct) signed on the left before you reach the village. Manned by dedicated volunteers, this is a small but informative set up where you can discover how the landscape was forged, learn about wherries which traded here, watch footage of early Broads' holiday life and see a fine collection of Broads' boats.

Horsey Windpump

Turn left on to the A149 and take the first right, following brown signs all the way to **Horsey Windpump ⓬**

Bure Valley Railway

Let the train take the strain and enjoy the views of Bure Valley from the narrow gauge railway which runs between Wroxham and the market town of Aylsham. This old-fashioned railway (www.bvrw.co.uk) operates from April to October, plus some winter weekends, with a journey time of 45 minutes. The train stops at Coltishall, Buxton and Brampton en route. You can also walk or pedal along the Valley Path that follows the railway.

Train and driver on the Bure Valley Railway

Horsey Windpump

(tel: 01263 740 241; www.national trust.org.uk; check website for opening times). The pump dates from 1912 and was restored in 1943 by the National Trust after damage by lightning. Climb to the top to enjoy fine views over the pretty **Horsey Mere**. After a bracing walk along the beach to see the seals (see page 46) the cosy *Nelson Head* pub in **Horsey** (see page 49) makes a welcome retreat.

Southern Broads

In comparison to their northern neighbours, the Southern Broads are less scenic with fewer facilities, but are also less crowded. The main road access is via Lowestoft, Norwich or **Loddon**, a lively little market town and boating centre on the River Chet. Many of the broads are inaccessible by car and you're better off going by boat, foot – or even train. **The Wherryman's Way** is the main long-distance footpath of the Broads (35 miles/56km) following the River Yare from Great Yarmouth

all the way to Norwich. From Great Yarmouth the path leads to the huge expanse of **Breydon Water**, a tidal estuary rather than a broad, revealing a vast expanse of mud at low tide. This gateway from the sea to the Broads is a haven for geese, ducks and waders – the RSPB have a nature reserve here with a bird hide.

Fine views over Breydon Water and Halvergate grazing marshes can be seen from the Roman fort remains of **Burgh Castle** (Tour 6, see page 53). The Wherryman's Way continues to **Berney Arms**, with a lofty windmill and wonderful views of the marshes and a remote pub (closed at time of writing). There is no road access but it has its own railway station. The path continues to **Reedham**, a busy spot renowned for its swing railway bridge and chain ferry for cars. This is the only place where you can cross the Yare between Great Yarmouth and Norwich so expect queues in summer. Further along the river is the minor but beautiful **Rockland Broad** and to the northwest **Surlingham**, popular for its pubs and walks in the Wheatfen Nature Reserve. The most southerly broad, and the one most easily accessible by car, is **Oulton Broad** (Tour 6, see page 54) near Lowestoft.

The *Electric Eel*

Explore a working marsh on the *Electric Eel* (June–Sept daily, April, May and Oct Sat & Sun, bank holidays, Easter week and half terms), departing from Toad Hole Cottage, How Hill, northeast of Horning. The electrically powered Edwardian-style boat glides through the dykes where reed and sedge are cut annually for thatch. Toad Hole Cottage, formerly an eel-catcher's cottage, is now an information point and study centre.

Eating Out

WOODBASTWICK
The Fur and Feather Inn
Slad Lane; tel: 01603 720 353;
www.woodfordes.com; food: daily
noon–9pm.

The tap for the neighbouring
Woodforde's Brewery, this is an
alluring thatched pub with top-notch
ales and home-made food.
Along with pub classics there are
puff pastry pies, such as venison
and merlot or pheasant and bacon,
plus a range of tasty burgers. Beer
fans can finish off with chocolate ale
cake flavoured with malted cream
and Norfolk Nog shooter. Be prepared
for a lighter summer menu. Bottled
beers, gifts and locally sourced
produce can be purchased from the
adjacent brewery. ££

WROXHAM
Wroxham Barns
Tunstead Road; tel: 01603 783 762;
www.wroxhambarns.co.uk; daily
10am–5pm.

Just north of Wroxham (and part of
the Wroxham Barns complex, see
page 44), this welcoming, award-
winning restaurant serves excellent
home-made snacks and lunches.
Try the chowder with locally
smoked haddock or the sausages
from the onsite company Scrummy
Pig, served with mash. And leave
room for the chocolate fondue.
£

HORSTEAD
The Recruiting Sergeant
Norwich Road; tel: 01603 737 077;
www.recruitingsergeant.co.uk; food:
Mon–Sat noon–2pm and 6.30–9pm (all
day in summer), Sun noon–4.30pm,
6–8.30pm.

In the village of Horstead, near
Coltishall, this gastropub is a great
place for locally caught fish and
seafood, Norfolk beef and pork and
Sunday roasts. The menu is more
sophisticated than the average Norfolk
pub, but you can just opt for fish and
chips. ££

HICKLING
The Greyhound Inn
The Green; tel: 01692 598 306;
www.greyhoundinn.com; food: daily
noon–8.30pm.

An alluring country pub with a good
choice of well-kept local and guest
real ales. Meat and seasonal
produce is locally sourced
wherever possible – Cromer crabs
are a favourite in summer. Meals can
be taken on the sunny front terrace,
in the cottage garden, by a roaring
fire or in the more formal dining
room. ££

HORNING
Bure River Cottage Restaurant
27 Lower Street; tel: 01692 631 421;
www.burerivercottagerestaurant.co.uk;
Tues–Sat 6–9pm.

A heaven for pescatarians. Start with
baked Cromer crab with chilli and
ginger and move on to pan-fried
local skate wing. Top it off with a
delicious dessert, such as ginger
panna cotta with roasted rhubarb.
££

HORSEY
Nelson Head
The Street; tel: 01493 393 378; food:
summer daily noon–9pm; winter
Mon–Fri noon–3pm and 6–8.30pm, Sat
noon–9pm, Sun noon–4pm.

This is a real traditional Norfolk pub,
where walkers, boaters and locals
are welcomed with local Woodforde's
ales, home-made meals, a roaring
fire in winter and a large garden
for summer. Unsurprisingly, Nelson
memorabilia forms part of the decor.
££

The Pleasure Beach,
Great Yarmouth

TOUR 6
Great Yarmouth

This 30-mile (48km) day tour of contrasts takes in the lively seaside resort of Great Yarmouth, as well as the peaceful landscape and cultural highlights inland.

Great Yarmouth used to be one of the wealthiest cities in the country. Before World War I over a thousand fishing trawlers were engaged in the industry, but over-fishing and competition from abroad led to a steep decline and the town today relies on servicing container ships, North Sea oil rigs and renewable energy sources. Yarmouth (as it used to be known) has been a seaside resort since 1760 and today boasts splendid sands and non-stop entertainment. It is a town of two very different parts: the holiday resort focussed on the marina, where golden sands are hidden from view behind the roller coasters, and the historic quarter of South Quay. Parking here can be tricky so leave the car along the seafront and walk across to the quayside.

Highlights

- Heritage Quarter and beach, Great Yarmouth
- Somerleyton Hall and Gardens
- Maritime Museum and South Beach, Lowestoft
- Oulton Broad

Great Yarmouth has recently restored a traditional part of its heritage – its winding Venetian waterways, an extensive planting scheme and a boating lake. It's set to attract a new crowd of tourists.

Heritage Quarter

The town's **Heritage Quarter** ❶ stretches along South Quay. Almost

The Town Hall and Heritage Quarter

opposite the Town Hall the *Lydia Eva* (www.lydiaevamincarlo.com; April–Oct Tues–Sun 10am–4pm; free) is the last surviving steam drifter of the herring fleet based in Great Yarmouth. A boat hand will show you round and talk nostalgically of the herring fleet in its heyday, when a drifter like the *Lydia Eva* would cast 65 nets out to sea. Cross the road for the **Elizabethan House Museum** (tel: 01493 855 746; www.nationaltrust.org.uk; April–Oct Sun–Fri 10am–

4pm), a much restored Tudor house built by a wealthy merchant and laid out to give you an idea of domestic life in the 16th century. Legend has it that a meeting to decide the fate of Charles I (death by execution) was held in the grander of the rooms, known as 'the Conspiracy Room'. Cromwell is said to have visited the house on several occasions.

You will find a series of narrow alleys known as **The Rows** which are originally separated medieval tenements. The alleys housed wealthy merchants at one end and bars and brothels at the other. Many of the Row houses were destroyed in World War II or demolished after the war, but the **Old Merchant's House** and **Row III** have been preserved. The nearby **Tolhouse** (tel: 01493 743 930; www.museums.norfolk.gov.uk; April–Oct daily 10am–4pm), once a medieval gaol, dwells on the fate of criminals and the tales of gaolers. Housing a museum since the 1880s, this ancient building looks strangely out of place among the modern houses and offices. There are plenty of

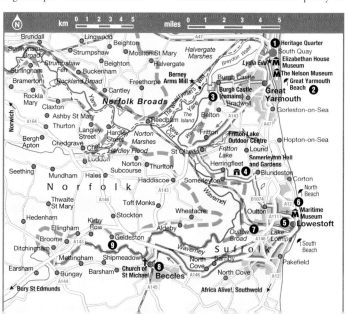

African animals

At Kessingland, south of Lowestoft, Africa Alive! (tel: 01502 740 291; www.africa-alive.co.uk; daily from 9.30am) presents the sights and sounds of Africa. Feed a meerkat, meet the aardvarks and see giraffes, zebras, lions, rhinos and many more species. There is ample to keep youngsters entertained including feeding and talks, a farmyard corner, a discovery centre and an adventure play area. Africa Alive! supports conservation projects in the wild to help secure the future of endangered species.

hands-on activities during the school holidays, often in conjunction with the Elizabethan House.

The nearby **Time and Tide Museum** (tel: 01493 743 930; www.museums.norfolk.gov.uk; early April–Oct daily 10am–4.30pm, Nov–March Mon–Fri 10am–4pm, Sat & Sun noon–4pm) covers the rise and decline of the fishing industry. The museum occupies the site of a Victorian herring curing works, where

Great Yarmouth rock for sale

the aroma of smoked fish still lingers. Homes of local fishermen and a 1950s fish wharf are recreated and visitors can take the wheel of a coastal drifter. In the Seaside Gallery a collection of postcards and posters, souvenirs and a 'What the Butler Saw' Mutoscope celebrate Great Yarmouth's heyday as a booming seaside resort. There are plenty of hands-on activities to keep children amused.

Marine parade

Be prepared for a neon-lit stretch of amusement arcades and a long row of garish attractions along the golden sands of **Great Yarmouth Beach ②**. If you have children in tow there are non-stop activities: rides and chutes on the beach; Pirates Cove mini-golf; the Merrivale Model Village, with its miniature garden railway and Old Penny Arcade; and the Sea Life aquarium. And if that's not enough there is always Pleasure Beach further south, with fairground rides galore. Alternatively just buy a bucket and spade for a good time on the golden sands.

The Royal Hotel

A few buildings along the front hint at Great Yarmouth's heyday. Opposite the Sea Life aquarium, the *Royal Hotel* dates back to the 18th century. It used to be called the Post House, as this was the pick-up point for the Royal Mail and also for passengers of the London Stage Coach. Dickens stayed here in 1848 and you can see a signed copy of his dinner menu hanging up in reception. Another famous guest was Edward VII, eldest son of Queen Victoria, who (according to the hotel) entertained his famous mistress here, the actress Lillie Langtry. Lillie made regular appearances on stage at the Royal Aquarium.

Children will love colourful Great Yarmouth Beach

Somerleyton Estate

Take the A143 going south, passing **Fritton Lake Outdoor Centre** (tel: 0333-456 0777; www.frittonlake. co.uk) on your left, an adventure centre offering residential holidays and pre-booked activities. To reach **Somerleyton Hall and Gardens** ❹ (tel: 0871 222 4244; www.somerleyton.co.uk; mid-April–Sept Tues, Thurs, Sun and public holidays 10am–5pm, gardens only on Wed), take the next turning left. A Victorian entrepreneur, Samuel Morton Peto, rebuilt this vast mansion in Tudor-Jacobean style. Peto went bankrupt and the house was sold to Sir Francis Crossley, whose family still own it. The interior features a splendid ballroom with white marble and crimson damask, but for many the highlight is the garden, incorporating a yew maze and a walled garden with glasshouses designed by Joseph Paxton (architect of London's Crystal Palace). From Somerleyton rejoin the B1074 going east for Lowestoft (6 miles/10km).

Lowestoft

England's most easterly town has seen better days. Once a thriving fishing port, **Lowestoft** ❺ now has no fishing fleet and the centre looks unloved and in much need of investment and revitalisation. The plus points are its golden **South Beach** and **Oulton Broad**. The glass East Point Pavilion is a striking building with a soft play centre and café. On Heritage Quay in the harbour, the *Mincarlo* (www.lydiaevamincarlo.com; normally Easter–Oct Tues–Sat 10am–3.30pm but check website for details; voluntary donation) is one of the few reminders of Lowestoft's heyday: the last of its sidewinder trawlers, built in 1961.

Burgh Castle

From Great Yarmouth take the Beccles Road, turning right at the roundabout before the road joins the A12. From here brown signs will direct you to **Burgh Castle** ❸ (tel: 0370 333 1181; www.english-heritage.org.uk; free). The impressive remains of the fort lie about 20 minutes' walk from the car park. This was one of nine forts on the Saxon Shore, built in AD 300 but probably abandoned 100 years later. The sheer size of the surviving walls is remarkable and the site, overlooking Breydon water and the surrounding marshes, is spectacular.

Dickens' Yarmouth

In 1848 Charles Dickens stayed at the *Royal Hotel* in Great Yarmouth with his colleague and friend, Mark Lemon, and was clearly impressed with the town as he used it as a main setting for *David Copperfield*. Peggotty, the Copperfields' faithful housekeeper, tells David it was a well-known fact that 'Yarmouth was, upon the whole, the finest place in the universe'.

The gardens at Somerleyton Hall

Lowestoft was built on the clifftops and in the early 19th century was famous for its 'hanging gardens' which cascaded from merchants' houses to the base of the cliffs. The merchants had fishing or shipbuilding businesses and used ancient thoroughfares known as scores, named after local characters or public inns, to get down to the north beach area. Some of the scores can still be seen today, while the best examples of Lowestoft's oldest houses, which survived World War II, can be seen along the High Street.

Scroby Sands

Scroby Sands Wind Farm, one of the UK's first commercial offshore wind farms, has the capability to supply 42,500 homes with energy. The visitor centre (June–Oct; free) has information on renewable energy. In summer, boat trips leave regularly from Great Yarmouth beach to see the seals who bask on Scroby Sands bank – look for chalked-up signs on the beach.

Maritime Museum

Lowestoft's excellent little **Maritime Museum** ❻ (tel: 01502 561 963; www.lowestoftmaritimemuseum.co.uk; mid-April–Oct daily 10am–5pm) is at the northern end of the resort, in a flint cottage below the lighthouse. From East Point Pavilion it's about 35 minutes on foot, or a short drive through the town. Displays cover Lowestoft's maritime history from fishing village to thriving port, with model boats, archive film footage and plenty of hands-on attractions for children.

Oulton Broad

Lowestoft has abundant aquatic attractions, but the most popular is **Oulton Broad** ❼, the southern gateway to the Broads, just 2 miles (3km) inland from Lowestoft beach. You can hire a self-drive boat for the day to explore the broad and the River Waveney or hop on the *Waveney Princess* (tel: 01502 574 903; www.waveney rivertours.com) for broad and river cruises. With sailings between April and October, you can glide through the Broadland landscape and maybe catch a glimpse of the elusive marsh harrier.

Beccles

From Lowestoft take the A146 to **Beccles ❽**. Formerly a flourishing Saxon sea port, it is today an appealing market town and the gateway to the Southern Broads. The dominant monument is the **Church of St Michael**, where Nelson's parents married. The handsome bell tower stands detached and offers far-reaching views from the top (guided tour only, enquire at the tourist office). Much of the activity in summer focuses on the marina, where you can feed the ducks, eat ice creams by the river or set off on a walk along the Marsh Trail. To discover the river take a trip on the *Big Dog* Ferry (tel: 07532 072 761; www.bigdogferry.co.uk), which stops off at **Geldeston ❾**.

Eating Out

GREAT YARMOUTH
Chico's Restaurant
60 Marine Parade; tel: 01493 856 222; chicosrestaurant.business.site; Wed–Sun 5–8.30pm.
There's plenty of bistro fare here along with an array of seafood choices.
What do you expect from a restaurant opposite the beach? Think mussels, prawn and cray fish cocktail and some giant crab claws. Meat eaters won't be disappointed either. Their fillet steak is a top choice. ££

SOMERLEYTON
The Duke's Head
Slugs Lane; tel: 01502 730 281; www.dukesheadsomerleyton.co.uk; food: Mon–Sat noon–2.30pm and 6.30–9pm, Sun noon–10.30pm.
This gastropub on the Somerleyton Estate (see page 53) places a strong emphasis on locally sourced produce, including Welsh black beef, Norfolk horn lamb and seasonal game from the estate. ££

OULTON BROAD
No. 142 Café & Bar
142 Bridge Road; tel: 07593 332 253; daily 9am–6pm.
Ideally located opposite Nicholas Everett Park at Oulton Broad, *No. 142 Café & Bar* delivers first-class treats for takeaway or to have in the café. The light lunch menu includes soup, a wide range of sandwiches, salads and jacket potatoes. You need to book for the full executive afternoon tea. The mocktails are delicious. £

BECCLES
Wine Vaults
2a Blyburgate; tel: 01502 713 381; www.winevaultsbeccles.co.uk; food: Mon–Fri noon–2.30pm and 6.30–9pm, Sat noon–9pm, Sun 10am–9pm.
Expect a warm welcome at this bar and restaurant in the heart of Beccles. The main menu offers sophisticated choices including dishes from the chargrill; the bar menu has good-value traditional meals – fish and chips, local sausages and steak and ale pie. ££

GELDESTON
The Wherry Inn
7 The Street; tel: 01508 518 371; www.wherryinn.co.uk; food: Mon noon–2.30pm, Tues–Thurs noon–2.30pm and 6–8pm, Fri & Sat noon–3pm and 6–8.30pm, Sun noon–6pm.
A cosy place to sit back next to a fireplace and enjoy some classic pub dishes. The Yorkshire puddings are huge, as is the battered catch of the day served with chips and mushy peas. Vegetarians can enjoy chargrilled vegetable kebabs and a mouth-watering pan-fried halloumi burger with salsa. Kids are well looked after with their own menu, and there's even a two-course lunch deal for pensioners on Mon, Wed and Fri. ££

BIRDWATCHING

The expertly managed nature reserves of Norfolk and Suffolk
offer the best birding in the UK and year-round activity,
including amazing flight displays of waders and wildfowl.

Even if you're not a keen birdwatcher,
the site of an elegant avocet skimming
the water or a flock of pink-footed
geese filling the skies might just
give you a momentary thrill. There's
plenty to see at any time of the year.
Wetlands and woodland, heathland
and coast provide a huge range
of habitats for both resident and
migratory species. There are some 100
nature reserves in the region, many
equipped with observation hides and
excellent visitor centres packed with

useful information on local wildlife,
trails, guided walks and the latest
sightings chalked up on boards.
    The Norfolk Broads are a haven for
wildlife. Look out for grebes, herons
and kingfishers. If you're very lucky
you may catch a glimpse of the shy
bittern or at least hear its strange
booming call. Hickling Broad, with
boat trips to hides, is the wildest of the
broads, its reedbeds and watermeadows
the haunt of bitterns, bearded tits and
marsh harriers. It's also one of the few

Twitchers at Dunwich Heath

the bird hides, some en route from the breeding grounds in the Arctic.

In Suffolk, the lovely Minsmere is the RSPB's flagship nature reserve, established in 1947 and known for marsh harriers, avocets, bearded tits, nightingales and bitterns. Book a boat trip here for Havergate Island, in the River Ore, famous for its breeding avocets and terns.

Birds to tweet about

Avocet The RSPB logo. A black and white wader, distinctive for its long upcurving beak. Its comeback from extinction in Britain was a great conservation victory in the 1940s.

Bearded tit Very pretty brown long-tailed bird with a distinctive 'ping' call but tricky to spot in the reeds.

Bittern Notoriously shy bird that hunts for fish, insects and frogs in reed beds. You're more likely to hear its distinctive booming call than see one.

Common crane Very rare in the UK, but in recent years up to 14 pairs have nested in the Norfolk Broads and two at Lakenheath Fen.

Lapwing Also known as a plover or peewit after its call. Distinctive crest. Endangered species.

Little tern Pretty, chattering seabird which has a distinctive yellow bill with black tip.

Marsh harrier Medium-sized bird of prey, mainly seen over reedbeds and marshes.

Pink-footed goose Produces high-pitched honking calls. Numbers are on the increase.

Stone curlew Crow-sized, with long yellow legs, largely nocturnal. Rarely seen – your best chance is Weeting Heath, Norfolk.

places you might spot a crane. On the north Norfolk coast, Cley Marshes Nature Reserve attracts a remarkable amount of birdlife all year round, including spotted redshank, avocet, spoonbills, oyster catchers, terns and grey plover. The reserve has a new eco-friendly visitor centre with panoramic views. In the café you can watch the birdlife through huge picture windows. Titchwell Marsh is another outstanding reserve, whose marshes, reed and beach bring thousands of migrating birds and a variety of species all year round.

In winter, spectacular flocks of waders and wildfowl make for the mudflats and lagoons of Snettisham Nature Reserve on The Wash. Just before high tide tens of thousands pack on to the banks and islands in front of

Punch and Judy show by Southwold Pier

TOUR 7
Southwold and Around

This 19-mile (31km) day-trip takes in picturesque Southwold, the quintessential English holiday resort, followed by coastal villages and Suffolk's top nature reserve.

This whole stretch of coast, characterized by sand and shingle beaches, marshland, dunes and crumbling cliffs, is designated as an Area of Outstanding Natural Beauty. The battle with coastal erosion has been going on for centuries and most of Dunwich has been washed away. Walking and birdwatching, especially at Minsmere, are popular pursuits and Southwold makes a great base for exploring the coast.

Southwold

A thriving fishing port in the 16th century, **Southwold** ❶ today is a remarkably unspoilt and charmingly old-fashioned, genteel sort of resort. Set on a clifftop and swept by stiff sea breezes, it is distinctive for its open greens, created after a fire destroyed

Highlights

- Southwold beach and pier
- Church of St Edmund, Southwold
- Holy Trinity Church, Blythburgh
- Dunwich Museum
- Minsmere RSPB Nature Reserve

most of the town in 1659. The town retains a variety of architectural styles: Georgian and Regency houses, Victorian seafront terraces, fishermen's cottages and buildings with a marked Dutch influence, reflecting trade with northern Europe. To the east, the sand and shingle beach is backed by the iconic Southwold beach huts; to the south, sailing and fishing boats are moored by the River Blyth. The

Southwold's famous beach huts

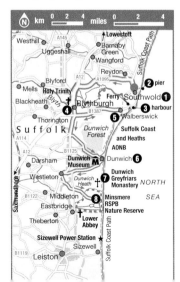

combination of seaside, enticing shops, restaurants, arts venues and wonderful walks and wildlife, have lured many a Londoner, and now around half of the town's houses are second homes.

Pier

At the north end of the beach, the retro **pier ❷**, with its cafés, shops and quirky amusements, is a focal point for both visitors and locals. It dates back to 1900 and has had a major revamp in recent years. Gimmicks range from traditional two-penny pushers to the eccentric Under the Pier Show, a wooden hut with slot machine inventions by local artist/engineer/ humourist Tim Hunkin – his 'Whack a Banker' game is the favourite. He also devised the ingenious water clock further along, which puts on a witty little show every hour or so.

Beach and harbour

Southwold's delightful beach huts, which fetch notoriously high prices (up to £120,000) overlook the sand and shingle beach. With fancy names like 'Chocolate Box' or 'Happy Days'

they are really no more than colourful seaside sheds, where you can make a cuppa or simple meal and store your buckets, spades and sunloungers. Just inland, the landlocked **lighthouse** (very occasional openings) dates from 1887 and still provides a waymark for vessels at night, visible for 15 miles (24km).

Right on the seafront is the **Southwold Sailors' Reading Room** (http://southwoldsailorsreadingroom. co.uk), a social club for retired sailors and fishermen, built in 1864 to deter them from taking to the bottle, fishing on Sundays or other unholy pursuits. This rather charming old-fashioned room, packed with maritime exhibits and open to the public (daily 9am–dusk), still provides a quiet retreat by the sea. To the far south lies Southwold's little **harbour ❸**, with sailing and fishing boats and shacks selling the catch of the day and seafood platters. A little rowing boat takes passengers, dogs and bikes across to Walberswick.

For a blast of adrenaline in sleepy Southwold take a half-hour trip around the bay on a speedy rigid inflatable boat with 12 wrap-around seats (tel: 07887 525 082; www.coastalvoyager. co.uk), departing from the harbour.

Sole Bay Inn, Southwold, known for its Adnams beers

Sole Bay Brewery

In the town centre follow your nose to the **Sole Bay Brewery** (tel: 01502 727 246; www.adnams.co.uk; daily tours, booking advised), where the malty wafts of brewing Adnams ale will greet you. Beer has been sold here since 1345, though the current brewery dates from 1872. Adnams became an integral part of Southwold, and brewery drays pulling carts packed with beer barrels were a familiar sight until 2006. Today's brewery boasts state-of-the-art machinery and is one of the greenest in the country. Friendly informative tours include a tutored tasting of beers as well as wine and gin – and a bottle of beer to take home. If you don't take the tour be sure to try the ale, available at any of the Southwold watering holes. You can also take a distillery tour or try the 'make your own gin' experience. Adnams goes from strength to strength, with a number of its own pubs and hotels, as well as a dozen Adnams Cellar & Kitchen stores. There is one round the corner on 4 Drayman Square, with the full range of Adnams beers, wines and spirits, attractive kitchenware and a good café.

Southwold Museum

Over the road from the shop, within a quaint gabled cottage, is the delightful **Southwold Museum** (tel: 01502 725 600; www.southwoldmuseum. org; April–Oct daily 2–4pm; free, but donations welcome) with special exhibits on the town's former fishing industry, its emergence as a prosperous seaside resort and the rise and decline of its railway. There's also a section on the bloody but indecisive Battle of Sole Bay, fought off the coast in 1672 between the combined British and French fleets against the Dutch.

Church of St Edmund

Just to the north, across Victoria Street, is the flint-faced, copper-roofed **Church of St Edmund**, one of Suffolk's finest late medieval churches and one of the few buildings to escape the devastating town fire of 1659. The interior is light and spacious, with carved, decorated angels on the roof, a rare painted rood-screen, finely carved choirs stalls and, on a plinth just beyond the font, the little armour-clad figure known as Southwold Jack, who used to strike the bell with his battle-axe to announce the start of services.

Carved angels in the roof of the Holy Trinity Church, Blythburgh

Holy Trinity Church, Blythburgh

From Southwold take the A1095 inland, turning left on to the A12 for Blythburgh. Bear left when you see the sign 'village only', then turn right for the **Holy Trinity Church** ❹. The wool trade of this previously prosperous port left its mark in 'the Cathedral of the Marshes' as it is known. The vast church soars majestically above the Blyth estuary

and can be seen for miles around. In a great storm in 1577 the church steeple crashed through the roof, killing two of the congregation. Some claim the visitor was the Devil, who left his scorch marks on the inside of the great north door. Another unwelcome visitor who left his mark was Puritan iconoclast, William Dowsing, who as Parliamentary Visitor to the Churches of Suffolk, smashed the windows and statues and left bullets in the timber roof. The church has beautifully carved angels decorating its tie-beam roof. Other distinctive features are the characterful poppyheads – carvings of little figures on the bench ends in the nave and the Blythburgh Jack-o'-the-Clock who once struck his bell on the hour and nowadays announces the entry of the clergy.

Walberswick

From Blythburgh take the B1125 south, shortly turning left on to the B1387 for the lovely village of **Walberswick** ❺. On the way into the village you'll pass **St Andrew's Church**, and the dramatic ruins beside it, which are evidence of the far grander building which once stood here. Walberswick

Picnic on the beach

The High Street in Southwold is a good place to pick up a picnic. The Black Olive Delicatessen at No. 80 has fabulous home-made pies, seafood products and local cheeses, as well as its namesake olives. Just along the road The Two Magpies Bakery produces artisan bread from scratch (watch the loaves being taken from the hearth ovens), filled foccaccia and irresistible *pâtisserie*. The drink has to be the local Adnams ales, from Adnams Cellar & Kitchen, round the corner from the brewery.

Beer for sale at Adnams Cellar & Kitchen

The Walberswick Ferry

Southwold to Walberswick by car is a trip of some 7 miles (11km), via Blythburgh and the A12. But pedestrians can get there in no time via the little bridge or Walberswick Ferry across the River Blyth. This is one of the few surviving rowed ferries in the UK, operated by the fifth generation of the same family. The boat runs in season only, carries up to 12 passengers, plus dogs and bikes, and takes just a couple of minutes.

Passengers board the Walberswick Ferry

today is a sleepy little village, and a favourite among artists for its beautiful coastal dunes, wild scenery and big skies (see page 102). It is also renowned for crabbing, especially on the little bridge at 'The Flats' where children dangle pieces of bacon on string to lure up the crustaceans. In 1981 Walberswick became the home of the grandly named British Open Crabbing Championship, drawing youngsters in their hundreds. The escalation of numbers put so much pressure on the organizers – and the stability of the local environment – that sadly the British Crabbing Federation had to terminate the event.

Dunwich

From Walberswick return along the B1387, turning left on to the B1125 towards Leiston. After just over a mile (2km) turn left and drive through Dunwich Forest for the coastal village of **Dunwich** ❻. Seeing the tiny village today it is hard to believe that this was the medieval capital of East Anglia and one of the largest ports in England, with six churches, two monasteries, two hospitals, major shipyards and a population which was one sixth that of London. Coastal erosion was checked for 200 years by the planting of

faggots, but in January 1286 a terrible storm deposited a million tonnes of sand and shingle into the harbour, destroying its status as a port. Further damage was caused by the storm of 1326 and the population plummeted to 600. Constant erosion over the centuries has reduced the village to a handful of houses, a pub, church and a beach with a café. The population of permanent residents is down to around 120. All that remains of medieval Dunwich are the ruins of the Leper

Relaxing on Walberswick beach

Dunwich Greyfriars Monastery

of the medieval **All Saints Church**, which fell into the sea in 1921. Legend has it that the sound of the church bells tolling from the sea bed can be heard when a storm is threatening.

The Dunwich Museum

The **Dunwich Museum** (tel: 01728 648 796; www.dunwichmuseum.org. uk; March Sat & Sun 2–4pm, April–Oct daily 11.30am–4.30pm; free, but donations welcome) charts the history of the town from Roman times to the present day. The most intriguing exhibit is the scale model of Dunwich in its heyday, showing all the medieval buildings that are under the waves. The rate of loss of land is roughly a yard/metre a year.

Chapel in the churchyard and those of the 13th-century **Dunwich Greyfriars Monastery** ❼ (www.dunwich greyfriars.org.uk; open year-round) on the clifftop just south of the village. This haunting monument is now managed by a charitable trust formed by local residents. A major restoration programme was completed in 2013 under the supervision of English Heritage. A solitary tombstone is the only testimony to the former presence

Dunwich Heath, south of the village, is a wide expanse of heather and scrubland, commanding splendid views of the coastline (marred only by the golfball-like Sizewell B nuclear power station to the south). The heath is owned by the National Trust and is known for birdlife, but for the best sightings go straight to the neighbouring Minsmere RSPB Nature Reserve (see page 64). For those who would like to walk but not necessarily

Latitude Festival

Offering endless entertainment for all the family, the Latitude Festival (www.latitudefestival.com) started in 2006 and is now one of the most popular festivals in East Anglia. It takes place over four days in July at Henham Park, an estate about 5 miles (8km) west of Southwold and offers a lively programme featuring music, comedy, theatre, dance, poetry and literature. Be prepared for traffic-clogged roads coming and going to the festival and book accommodation a year ahead.

Young revellers in the woods at Latitude Festival

Beautiful Dunwich Heath

in the fee-paying reserve, there is a well-marked, easy-going 5-mile (8km) footpath encircling Minsmere, taking in heath, beach, marshland and woodland, and involving just 500yds/metres on a public road.

You can leave the car at the National Trust's Coastguard Cottages (car park charge for non-members), which have excellent tearooms, at Dunwich Heath; alternatively, you could start the walk at *The Eel's Foot Inn* at Eastbridge.

George Orwell

Eric Arthur Blair's family home was in Southwold and the author came back to live here in 1929–35. It was in here that he wrote his experimental novel *A Clergyman's Daughter*, the inspiration of which may have been the clergyman's daughter, Brenda Salkeld, the gym teacher at the local St Felix School, whom he fell for. In 1933 he published his more famous novel, *Down and Out in Paris and London* under the name of George Orwell – taking his surname from Suffolk's River Orwell that he so loved.

Minsmere RSPB Nature Reserve

To reach Minsmere from Dunwich village by car, drive to Westleton, and follow the brown sign off the green for Minsmere. It's about 2.5 miles (4km) along a narrow road, through some beautiful woodland. You don't have to be a birdwatcher to enjoy the coastal and woodland trails at the **Minsmere RSPB Nature Reserve** ❽ (tel: 01728 648 281; www.rspb.org. uk; reserve: daily dawn–dusk; Visitor Centre: Feb–Oct 9am–5pm, Nov–Jan 9am–4pm) but it helps to enjoy nature as this is one of the best spots in the UK for wildlife. It opened in 1947 and has become increasingly popular, particularly since hosting the BBC2 wildlife series *Springwatch*.

The diverse habitats are home to an astonishing variety of birds and other wildlife. In spring and summer you might spot an avocet skimming the water, a marsh harrier 'dancing' above the reed beds, hear the deep booming call of the bittern or catch a glimpse of a shy otter or red deer. Look out too for terns, oystercatchers and lapwings or, among the most endangered species, nightjars and bearded tits.

This is a well-organized reserve with a helpful visitor centre, waymarked circular trails, hides overlooking lagoons and reed beds, guides on hand to tell you what to look out for and binoculars to hire. Youngsters can have fun in the Wild Zone, building a den or joining in summer activities such as pond dipping and owl pellet dissection. There's a good shop too and a café with great bacon butties and home-made bread pudding and scones.

Eating Out

SOUTHWOLD

Lord Nelson

East Street; tel: 01502 722 079; www.thelordnelsonsouthwold.co.uk; food: daily noon–2pm and 6.30–9pm. A Southwold institution. It's cosy, close to the sea and, unsurprisingly, serves the full selection of the local Adnams beers. Expect tasty home-cooked dishes (fish and chips, Thai green curry, Norfolk mussels). The enclosed flower-decked garden is perfect for alfresco meals. ££

Sole Bay Fish Co.

Shed 22e Blackshore; tel: 01502 724 241; www.solebayfishco.co.uk; daily noon–3pm.
You can't get fresher than this, with produce straight off the owners' boats or smoked in their own smokehouse. Now a fully licensed restaurant, this is a great place to come for a unique lunch experience. Fresh fish sold daily (8am–4.30pm). ££

Southwold Boating Lake and Tearoom

North Road; tel: 07771 781 739; www.southwoldboatinglakeandtearoom.co.uk; Easter–mid-Oct Mon–Fri 11am–3.30pm, Sat & Sun 10am–4pm.
Friendly, 1940s-style lakeside café. You can enjoy light lunches or scrumptious cream teas sitting on Lloyd loom chairs on the lakeside verandah (warm fleecy blankets are provided if it's cool) or in the quirky little tea room. £

Sutherland House

56 High Street; tel: 01502 724 544; www.sutherlandhouse.co.uk; Tues–Sun noon–2pm and 7–9pm.
Smart hotel restaurant where food miles are given on the menu and only seasonal ingredients are used. Try the freshly caught fish, 28-day aged steak or carrot and coriander fritters. There's also a set lunch menu (£). £££

WALBERSWICK

The Bell Inn

Ferry Road; tel: 01502 723 109; www.bellinnwalberswick.co.uk; food daily noon–2.30pm and 6–9pm.
Ancient village pub with views over the dunes and harbour from its large garden. Decent home-made pub grub includes starters such as Suffolk smokies and mains like steak, ale and mushroom pie. ££

DUNWICH

Dingle Hill Tearooms

Dingle Hill; tel: 01728 648 872; www.dinglehilltearooms.co.uk; Mon–Fri 10am–5pm, Sat & Sun 9am–4pm.
This charming tearoom, which prides itself on cakes, scones, sandwiches and quiches freshly made on site, is hidden away alongside a small garden nursery. Take the road opposite the church and it's on your right. £

The Ship at Dunwich

St James Street; tel: 01728 648 219; www.shipatdunwich.co.uk; food: Mon–Fri 8–10am, noon–3pm and 6–9pm, Sat & Sun and school holidays 8–10am, noon–9pm.
This former smugglers' haunt, which is also a hotel, has a cosy atmosphere and good locally sourced food. Expect home-smoked fish, ham hock and pork belly from Blythburgh and Suffolk cheeseboard. ££

TOUR 8

Aldeburgh and Around

This full-day 25-mile (40km) tour follows in the footsteps of Benjamin Britten at the well-to-do resort of Aldeburgh, then heads inland to Snape Maltings and historic sites nearby.

Aldeburgh is a prosperous little town and seaside resort, with the charm of a bygone era. The town acquired international fame through the music festival, held here until 1967 when new premises were acquired at Snape. But Aldeburgh is still very much a festival centre, hosting concerts and exhibitions and accommodating Snape audiences. The composer Benjamin Britten (1913–76) spent most of his adult life in or near Aldeburgh and it was here that he wrote some of the best-known classical music of the 20th century and founded the Aldeburgh Festival (see page 74) with Peter Pears. With its shingle beach, boats and fish huts, Aldeburgh is a delightful spot to stay and has an exceptionally good choice of accommodation and

Highlights

- Aldeburgh
- Snape Maltings
- Orford Castle
- Sutton Hoo
- Woodbridge Tide Mill

restaurants. If you have more than a day, this route could be linked to Tour 7 (see page 58), covering the coast to the north.

Aldeburgh

Parking in the centre of **Aldeburgh** ❶ can be tricky, but there are car parks on Thorpe Road to the north (charge) and Slaughden Quay to the south (free). Start on the waterfront at the lovely,

The Tudor Moot Hall in Aldeburgh

fish are sold from the huts on the steeply shelving shingle beach.

Just south of the Moot Hall, **Crag House** at 4 Crabbe Street was Benjamin Britten's seafront home from 1947–57. On the same street, Jubilee Hall is a venue for concerts, the poetry festival and summer theatre.

Along Crag Path, with desirable residences right on the seafront, you'll find the **Aldeburgh Beach Lookout** tower, a quirky 19th-century folly, which was sold with the proviso it must be used for artistic purposes. Sir Laurens van der Post used to write here in his later years, in the tiny room half way up. The tower was bought by Caroline Wisemen, an international art dealer who was inspired by Aldeburgh and who has turned the tower into a place where established and emerging artists can also come and be inspired by the Aldeburgh coastline. Exhibitions are held here (and in the house across the road) and Caroline offers week-long residences at the Lookout – at the end of the week their creations are revealed to the public at the tower. The Aldeburgh Academy, run by David

brick and timber-framed **Moot Hall**, a fine Tudor building that formerly stood well inland from the sea. A symbol of Aldeburgh, it has been a venue for council meetings for over 400 years and houses a small museum (daily April–Oct 2.30–5pm, June–Aug from noon). Along the seafront fishermen land their glistening catch and fresh

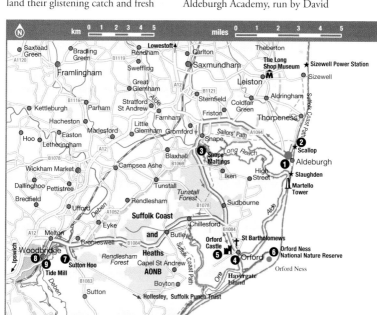

Baldry, offers three-day art courses during the summer months.

Running parallel with the sea, the **High Street** retains many independent shops, with appealing galleries, boutiques, delis and a wonderful book shop. Carry on walking south and you come to the clover-shaped **Martello Tower**, built, like many along the East coast, in preparation for Napoleonic attacks – which never happened. It's a great place to watch the sea and can be rented as self-catering accommodation through the Landmark Trust (www.landmarktrust.org.uk).

Maggi Hambling's Scallop

A short walk north along the beach from the Moot Hall brings you to Maggi Hambling's huge steel *Scallop* ❷, dedicated to Benjamin Britten. On a heritage coast where little has changed over the years, the sculpture was a hotly controversial topic when unveiled in 2003. It has been subject to graffiti and vandalism, though the attacks have abated in recent years. Locals are still divided over its aesthetic merit but it has become something of a magnet for visitors, especially for snap-happy tourists and children who

like to hide behind the interlocking shells – rather than contemplating the mysterious power of the sea, which Maggi Hambling intended. If nothing else, *Scallop* is a great talking point and provides excellent photo opportunities – it looks different from every angle and changes colour as you look at it. The words that are pierced through the steel and read against the sky – 'I hear those voices that will not be drowned' – come from Britten's opera *Peter Grimes*.

Thorpeness

A 30-minute walk or a couple of minutes' car journey along the narrow coastal road north of Aldeburgh will bring you to **Thorpeness**. This was just a fishing hamlet until it was transformed in the 1920s into a fantasy holiday haven, with a boating lake and Peter Pan-themed islands, a fairytale cottage on stilts, a country club and mock Tudor and Jacobean homes. It even had its own railway station. The entrepreneur behind the scheme was Glencairn Stuart Ogilvie, a Scottish lawyer and playwright. It was hailed as the new Suffolk seaside resort and is still very much a holiday

Maggi Hambling's *Scallop* on Aldeburgh beach

A room with a view – the *House in the Clouds*, Thorpeness

attraction with its 64-acre (25-hectare) boating lake, golf course and the *House in the Clouds*, perched on top of a water tower, and available for self-caterers who like a view.

Snape Maltings

From Aldeburgh take the A1094 heading inland, turning left for Snape after about 4 miles (6km). Formerly one of the largest barley maltings in East Anglia, Snape ceased operation in the 1960s. The 19th-century

complex of red-brick granaries and malt houses beside the Alde estuary were converted by Benjamin Britten into a concert hall and the Aldeburgh Festival has been held here ever since. For information and booking for the year-round concert hall programme visit www.snapemaltings.co.uk.

Snape Maltings ❸ (tel: 01728 688 303; www.snapemaltings.co.uk; daily 10am–5.30pm) today is a 7-acre (3-hectare) site overlooking wildlife-rich reed beds. It's a beautiful setting, with grounds enhanced by modern sculpture, including striking works by Henry Moore and Barbara Hepworth. Snape now has a nature reserve with walks along the River Alde and boat trips in season. The shops in the converted granaries are alone worth a visit. On the food scene it has an artisan bakery, a gourmet deli, an excellent café, the Granary tearooms, a pub and a wonderful farmers' market held every first Saturday of the month (9.30am–1pm). It is also the venue of the annual Aldeburgh Food and Drink Festival, held in the autumn. Other shops include classy boutiques, children's toys and clothes, fine furnishings, kitchenware, pottery, crafts and cards.

Long Shop Museum

Northwest of Aldeburgh, Leiston's Long Shop Museum (www.longshop museum.co.uk; Mon–Sat 10am–5pm, Sun 11am–3pm) is the site of the Leiston Works, which turned the town into a prosperous manufacturing centre in the 19th century. The works were owned by Richard Garrett & Sons, who made steam tractors, cast-metal products and munitions for both World Wars. The museum charts 200 years of machinery and includes displays on the nuclear power stations at nearby Sizewell.

Vintage machinery on display at the Long Shop Museum

Orford

From Snape Maltings take the Snape
Road south via Sudbourne to Orford
(5.5 miles/9km). Once a thriving port
and town, **Orford ❹** is a mere village
dominated by the mighty keep of the
former **Orford Castle ❺** (tel: 01394
450 472; www.english-heritage.org.uk;
April–Sept daily 10am–6pm, Oct daily
10am–5pm, Nov–March Sat & Sun
10am–4pm). The military stronghold
was built by Henry II as part of a
series of coastal defences in 1165. The
gradual formation by the North Sea of
the shingle spit (Orford Ness) led to
the demise of the port and the decline
of what were originally extensive castle
fortifications. The castle became home
to coastal defences during World War
II in its life as a radar station. The
90ft (27-metre) -high keep, the oldest
five-sided keep in the country, soars
above the village, and the top of the
tower (91 steps) commands great views
across to Orford Ness.

The nearby **Church of St
Bartholomew**, vast in proportion to
today's village, was the setting of some
of the early performances by Benjamin
Britten, and concerts are held here
during the Aldeburgh Festival. Orford
may be tiny but it is something of a

Orford Castle

foodie haven, famous for seafood and
home to an oysterage, a smokehouse,
a scratch bakery and Suffolk butcher,
two pubs and riverside tearooms with
home-made cakes. A further lure
is the *Crown and Castle*, now a bed
and breakfast with 21 rooms, whose
Trinity Restaurant serves up decent,
unpretentious food. Pinney's of
Orford, dating from the 1950s, has a
shop near the quay. Their oyster beds
and smokehouse are down on Butley
Creek and their products are used at
their excellent restaurant, *Butley Orford
Oysterage*, which opened in 1961 (see
page 73).

The road past the old *Jolly Sailor
Inn* leads to **Orford Quay** with a
hut selling fresh fish, a simple café
and, weather permitting, boat trips
to Havergate Island to see avocets
and other waders. Ferries take
passengers from here to **Orford
Ness National Nature Reserve ❻**
(www.nationaltrust.org.uk), a desolate
10-mile (16km) shingle spit known for
breeding and migratory birds. From
1913 to the mid-1980s the Ness was
used as a military test site carrying out
secret experiments. Derelict concrete
buildings used for the testing are the
legacy of this secret era.

Dining on the Alde

Spot the avocets and learn about local
wildlife on the *Lady Florence* (tel:
07831 698 298; www.lady-florence.
co.uk), a 1940s Admiralty MFV supply
boat. Trips start at Orford, cruise the
length of the Orford Ness conservation
area and circumnavigate the RSPB's
Havergate Island bird sanctuary. The
maximum number of passengers is
12, there's a comfy salon, a coal fire in
winter and a choice of brunch, lunch,
dinner or sunset cocktail cruises, all at
reasonable prices.

Ipswich

From Woodbridge it's only 9 miles (15km) to Ipswich, the county town of Suffolk. It is a large town with unappealing outskirts, but it now has a regenerated waterfront where you can sit at cafés and watch the yachts, or take a cruise along the River Orwell. Christchurch Mansion in the eponymous park is a handsome Tudor building with a good collection of paintings by Constable and Gainsborough.

Ipswich's regenerated waterfront and harbour

Sutton Hoo

From Orford take the B1084 west towards Woodbridge. After 9 miles (15km) turn left on to the B1083 for **Sutton Hoo** ❼ (tel: 01394 389 700; www.nationaltrust.org.uk; April–Oct daily 10.30am–5pm, Nov–March Sat & Sun 11am–4pm), one of the country's most significant Anglo-Saxon sites. In 1939, just before World War II, the landowner, Mrs Edith Pretty, asked amateur archaeologist, Basil Brown, to excavate the grassy mounds on her land. The dig revealed the

Anglo-Saxon shield replica at Sutton Hoo

rotting timbers of an 89ft (27-metre) long ship, thought to have been used as the burial chamber of the Saxon King Raedwald of East Anglia in the 7th century. The ship was packed with the most priceless hoard of Anglo-Saxon treasure ever discovered. Sadly you can't see it here as it was taken to the British Museum for safekeeping.

The site nevertheless has a fascinating exhibition, with replicas of the treasure, including the famous silver and gold ceremonial helmet which is the symbol of Sutton Hoo. The audio-guides feature Basil Brown himself describing the dig. Visitors can see the reconstructed burial chamber, visit some of the rooms in Mrs Pretty's house, with interesting correspondence about the discovery, and wander around burial mounds. It's a beautiful site: 245 acres (99 hectares) above the River Deben, with woodland and estuary walks. The one-hour guided tours of the burial mounds are highly recommended but, with or without the tour, allow at least a couple of hours for the whole site.

Woodbridge

The unspoilt town of **Woodbridge** ❽ lies just across the River Deben. From Sutton Hoo take the B1083 north, and

The Suffolk Punch Trust

At the village of Hollesley, southeast of Woodbridge, the Suffolk Punch Trust (tel: 01394 411 327; www.suffolkpunchtrust.org; check website for opening hours) is an educational and environmental charity dedicated to breeding and preserving the Suffolk Punch horse and its links with East Anglia's rural heritage. There's plenty for children, with stallions, mares and foals, along with rare breeds of pigs, sheep and chickens, a play area, garden, country walks and a good café.

A Suffolk Punch in the snow

turn left at the roundabout on to the A1152. In Tudor times the town was a flourishing centre for shipbuilding, sail-making and weaving. Large boats can no longer navigate the River Deben, but this is still a favourite spot among the boating fraternity, with much of the activity focussing on the busy quayside and yacht harbour. It's also a delightful market town, full of small retailers (its slogan is 'Choose Woodbridge for real shopping') and a haven for gourmets with many tempting delis, cafés and restaurants.

The Tide Mill

On the River Deben quayside lies the white clapboard **Tide Mill** ❾ (Tide Mill Way; tel: 01394 388 202; www.woodbridgetidemill.org.uk; April–Sept daily 11am–4.30pm, Oct weekends only). The nearest car park is at the railway station just to the west. The mill dates from the 1790s, though the site was first mentioned in 1170. Functioning until 1957 it was the last mill in the country to work by tidal power.

Explore the fully restored and working tide mill, plus exhibits and interactive models presenting

an overview of the history and workings of the mill. From here you can follow a riverside walk in either direction, offering the chance to spot oystercatchers, terns, shelduck, avocet and, if you are really lucky, one of the 'Deben seals'.

Narrow streets lead up from the quay to the town centre, well worth exploring for its Georgian streets, galleries, shops and charming **Market Hill**. The Dutch gabled Shire Hall (1575) was formerly used on the upper level as a Magistrates' Court and the ground floor as an open corn market. The little museum across the road has displays on the evolution of Woodbridge from the Anglo-Saxon settlement to the 20th century.

The white clapboard Tide Mill in Woodbridge

Eating Out

ALDEBURGH

Aldeburgh Fish & Chip Shop

226 High Street; tel: 01728 452 250; www.aldeburghfishandchips.co.uk; Mon–Thurs noon–2pm and 6–8pm, Sat noon–8pm.

This takeaway chippie's fame has spread far and wide and some argue it's the best in the country. The fish and potatoes are local, the batter is light. All in all, it's well worth the long wait. £

The Lighthouse

77 High Street; tel: 01728 453 377; www.lighthouserestaurant.co.uk; daily noon–2pm and 6.30–10pm.

A favourite haunt of locals. Fish predominates on the menu, with pan-seared scallops, Lighthouse fish soup, oven-baked cod fillets and seabass, but there are always a couple of dishes for keen carnivores. A busy, bustling atmosphere. ££

Regatta Restaurant

171 High Street; tel: 01728 452 011; www.regattaaldeburgh.com; Tues–Sat noon–2pm and 6–9pm, also Sun & Mon in summer school holidays.

Cheerful, family-run restaurant with a nautical theme that delivers dishes full of flavour and features recipes from their own smokehouse. There's an emphasis on fish and seafood but plenty of other options – meat and vegetarian. ££

THORPENESS

The Kitchen@Thorpeness

Remembrance Road; tel: 01728 453 266; www.thekitchenthorpeness. co.uk; Sun–Thurs 9am–5pm, Fri & Sat until 8pm.

Just across the road from the Meare, you'll find the perfect spot for coffee, home-made cakes, chunky sandwiches and super lunches. Have a wander around the Emporium for collectables and crafts afterwards. £

SNAPE

Crown Inn

Bridge Road; tel: 01728 688 324; food: Mon–Fri noon–2.30pm and 6–9.30pm, Sat & Sun noon–3pm and 6–9pm.

You can be assured of locally grown produce at this 15th-century inn. Garry and Teresa Cook rear geese, ducks, Suffolk lamb, rare breed pigs and goats, plus the veg is from their allotment at Orford. The local brewery Adnams supplies the ales. Pre- and post-concert meals available. ££

ORFORD

Butley Orford Oysterage

Market Hill; tel: 01394 450 277; www.pinneysoforford.co.uk; daily noon–2.15pm, also 6.30–9pm seasonally so check in advance.

This long-established seafood restaurant has its own smokehouse and two boats which provide a variety of locally caught fish. Try the plump Butley Creek oysters, home-made smoked salmon paté, creamy fish pie or catch of the day. They also have a shop near the harbour called Pinney's. ££

WOODBRIDGE

The Table

3 Quay Street; tel: 01394 382 007; www.thetablewoodbridge.co.uk; Mon 10.30am–3pm, Tues–Sat 10.30am–3pm and 6–9pm, Sun noon–3pm.

This brasserie-style restaurant is set in a lovely old building with a courtyard for summer eating. Choose from light fresh bites or mains such as Thai chicken curry or smoked haddock soufflé; veggies are well catered for too. Or stop by for coffee and yummy home-made cakes. ££

ALDEBURGH FESTIVAL

'If wind and water could write music, it would sound like Ben's':
Yehudi Menuhin referring to the great British composer, Benjamin
Britten, who founded the world-famous music festival.

Inspired by the vast skies and ever-changing seas of the Suffolk coast, the great British composer Benjamin Britten (1912–76) lived and worked in Aldeburgh for 20 years. He was born in Lowestoft, where he started composing from a very young age, then attended Gresham's School in Holt, Norfolk, and went on to the Royal College of Music. Britten was a lifelong pacifist and in 1939 he fled to America as a conscientious objector with the tenor, Peter Pears, his partner

in both professional and private life, returning to Aldeburgh after the war. Britten and Pears lived together at Crag House in Aldeburgh but as their fame spread the house in the centre on the seafront became too much of a public attraction and they sought solitude in the more peaceful Red House, a mile from the centre.

In 1948 Britten founded the Aldeburgh Festival with Pears and the librettist Eric Crozier, which was at first, 'a modest festival with a few

Grimes on the Beach, performed at the Aldeburgh Festival

also attend the Snape Proms in August and other events throughout the year.

Snape Maltings has other year-round attractions: stylish independent shops and several cafés converted from riverside buildings, a fine nature reserve and guided walks by the RSPB.

Britten's legacy

Church of St Peter and St Paul (Church Close, above the town) Graves of Benjamin Britten and Peter Pears; Britten memorial window designed by John Piper.

Moot Hall The Tudor building next to the beach was the setting for the opening scene of Peter *Grimes*.

Crag House, 4 Crabbe Street. Britten's home from 1947–57.

Aldeburgh Jubilee Hall, Crabbe Street. The earliest venue for the festival, and still used for events.

Peter Pears Gallery, 152 High Street. Main gallery for Aldeburgh Festival exhibitions.

Scallop On the northern beach, Maggie Hambling's controversial sculpture is dedicated to Britten. The words cut into the shell 'I hear those voices that will not be drowned' are from *Peter Grimes*.

The Red House, Golf Lane (tel: 01728 687 110; www.brittenpears.org; April–Oct Tues–Sat 1–5pm; guided tours (45 minutes) Tues–Sat 2pm, booking required; Oct–mid-Dec Tues–Fri 2–5pm, gallery and studio only. The house where Britten and Pears lived from 1957, now home to the Britten-Pears Foundation.

Snape Maltings Concert Hall operated by Aldeburgh Music, as well as stylish shops and galleries.

concerts given by friends'. Soon it was bringing together international stars and emerging talent.

Initially, the festival used local venues, but in 1967 they converted a Victorian maltings in Snape into a 830-seat concert hall. It is now the home of Aldeburgh Music, which has a world-wide reputation as a performance centre and offers a year-round programme of artist development and education.

The festival, held in June each year, goes from strength to strength and ranks among the finest music festivals in the world. The 17-day-long extravaganza is packed full of contemporary and classical music, comedy, drama, poetry and art exhibitions, but the key works are always Britten's operas. Audiences can

St Edmund's Abbey ruins

TOUR 9
Bury St Edmunds and Around

On this full-day, 37-mile (59km) driving tour, discover the historic sites of elegant Bury St Edmunds and the enticing villages of the Stour Valley to the south.

The ancient market town of Bury St Edmunds was named after Edmund, the last Saxon king of East Anglia who was slain by the Danes in 869 at Hoxne on the Norfolk border. His body was brought here for reburial in 903 and pilgrims came to worship at his shrine. Today Bury is a bustling market town, with monastic ruins and a large number of historic buildings. From here it is a short drive to the beautiful villages of the Stour Valley which owe their splendour to the wool trade that flourished in former times.

Bury St Edmunds

One of East Anglia's finest towns, **Bury St Edmunds ❶** retains Georgian and Victorian buildings, immaculate gardens and sufficient ruins to give you

Highlights

- Bury St Edmunds
- Ickworth House
- Cavendish
- Long Melford
- Lavenham

some idea of the scale and splendour of its former abbey. It's also a foodie's delight with more than its fair share of tempting cafés and eateries.

Start in the centre at **Angel Hill**, a square of Georgian and other buildings, overlooked by the ivy-clad ***Angel Hotel***. It was here that Charles Dickens gave readings from *Nicholas Nickleby* and *David Copperfield*. He stayed at the inn in 1835, 1859

Statue of St Edmund in the Abbey Gardens

and 1861 and was pleased with the 'handsome little town of cleanly and thriving appearance' – so much so that he organized for Mr Pickwick to visit the town a few years later. Today the *Angel* is a four-star boutique hotel and restaurant. On the south side the square is bordered by the **Athenaeum**, hub of social life in Georgian times.

Off Angel Hill are the immaculate and colourful **Abbey Gardens** (Mon–Sat 7.30am–dusk, Sun 9am–dusk; free) created within the walls of the former medieval monastery. Beyond the neat flower beds are the **ruins of St Edmund's Abbey**, in some cases mere mounds of rubble. The most substantial ruins are those lying behind the neighbouring Cathedral. The abbey was named after King Edmund, who was buried here, and in the Middle Ages it became one of the richest Benedictine foundations in England. It was here in 1214 that 25 barons swore to exact their rights from King John, leading to the signing of Magna Carta the following year. In 1327 the abbey was sacked by

the townspeople in a protest against monastic control and the Abbey Gate was destroyed. In 1539 the abbey was dissolved and most of the buildings dismantled. The finely preserved **gatehouse** at the entrance of the gardens dates from 1347.

St Edmundsbury Cathedral

The church you see today dates back to the 15th century but was only granted cathedral status in 1914. The Gothic-style tower lantern (seen from the far end of the nave) was built in 2005 with a grant from the Millennium Commission and local fund-raising. The tower has become a new city landmark. Exiting the cathedral you pass the **Norman Tower**, built as the main gatehouse to the abbey precincts.

St Mary's Church

Next along is **St Mary's Church** (Mon–Sat 9am–4pm, until 3pm in winter), built between 1290 and 1490 as part of the abbey complex. The finest feature is the hammer-beam

The ornate interior of the Corn Exchange, which is now a pub

roof, with 11 pairs of large angels, attended by lesser angels on the wall plates, and a procession of saints, martyrs, prophets and kings. It's difficult to see the detail of the dark wood but the mirrored trolley helps, or you can ask for the lights to be switched on. Behind the altar at the far end of the church lies the very simple tomb of Mary Tudor, sister of Henry

An exhibit at the Moyse's Hall Museum

VIII. Her remains were brought here from the abbey after the Reformation.

Greene King Brewery

You will soon come to the **Greene King Brewery** (tel: 01284 714 297; www.greeneking.co.uk; guided tours Mon & Tues 2pm, Wed–Fri 11am and 2pm, Sat 11am, 12.30pm, 2pm and 3.30pm, Sun 11.30pm). Greene King has been brewing in Bury St Edmunds since 1799 and a guided tour gives you an interesting insight into the whole brewing process. The tour includes views of the town from the roof of the Art Deco Brew House and tutored tastings of the full range of beers in the Beer Café.

Opposite the brewery, the delightful **Theatre Royal** (tel: 01284 769 505; www.theatreroyal.org) is the last remaining Regency-era playhouse in the country. It is run by the National Trust and puts on a lively programme of professional and community performances.

Abbeygate and Cornhill

Return to Abbey Hill and walk up Abbeygate, a busy shopping street, to

The Greene King Brewery

the **Cornhill** and **Buttermarket**. The neoclassical **Corn Exchange** is the predominant building, now occupied by a Wetherspoon pub. Across the Cornhill **Moyse's Hall Museum** is one of Britain's last surviving Norman houses; today it's a tourist information spot and a small town museum. Bury's market on the Cornhill and Buttermarket on Wednesday and Saturday mornings is a colourful affair and one of the best in the region. West of here, **The Arc** is the town's latest (and controversial) shopping centre,

also home to the Apex entertainment centre.

Ickworth House

From Bury take the A143 southwest towards Haverhill. At Horringer follow the signs for **Ickworth House ❷** (tel: 01284 735 270; www.national trust.org.uk; house: mid-March–Oct Thurs–Tues 11am–5pm, also Wed in school hols, Nov & Dec daily 11am–3pm, garden and park: daily 9am–5.30pm, until 4.30pm Nov & Dec). The estate is worth visiting for the grounds alone, with eight waymarked trails for walking and cycling. The neoclassical design of the house, comprising a huge rotunda with wings connected by curving corridors, was conceived in 1795 by the eccentric Frederick Hervey, 4th Earl of Bristol. 'When God created the human race, he made men, women and Herveys'. Attributed to Voltaire, the quote refers to the second Lord Hervey but has been used for subsequent and equally unconventional Herveys who have lived here. (The information plaques along the terrace will put you in the picture.)

Today the estate is run by the National Trust. State rooms in the rotunda are richly furnished, with

---

Pint-sized pub

The quaint *Nutshell* pub, by the Corn Exchange in Bury St Edmunds, has made the *Guinness World Records* as the smallest pub in the country. If you want a pint, bear in mind there's only room for around a dozen drinkers – and no space for food. One of the famous curiosities within the olde-worlde interior is the mummified black cat hanging above the bar that was found during restoration work.

The landlord of *The Nutshell*, Britain's smallest pub

Local crafts and gifts

vast sparkling chandeliers (each one costing £3,000 to clean!), fine portraits by Reynolds, Gainsborough and Velazquez, and a stunning collection of Georgian silver. The servants' basement gives you a good insight into downstairs life in the 1930s.

Clare and Cavendish

Turning right out of Ickworth follow the A143 for 8 miles (13km) and turn left at Stradishall (B1063), signed to **Clare ❸**. The village lies 5 miles (8km) along this road, its centre dominated by the splendid 'wool' **Church of St Peter and St Paul**. One of Suffolk's best examples of pargetting can be seen on the quaint **Ancient House** (the local museum) opposite the south porch of the church. Vestiges of the Norman keep and the old railway station buildings lie within the 25-acre (10-hectare) **Castle Country Park**, the starting point for waymarked walks.

Follow the A1092 east to the village of **Cavendish ❹**. The scene of pink thatched cottages flanking the green, and the medieval church tower rising behind, is one of the most photographed in East Anglia. In more

turbulent times Wat Tyler, leader of the Peasants' Revolt in 1381, was killed at Smithfield by John Cavendish, arch enemy of the peasants, who lived in a house on the green. Cavendish was then beheaded in Bury St Edmunds by Tyler's supporters.

Long Melford

Continue 4 miles (7km) along the A1092 for **Long Melford ❺**. The village derives its name from a former mill and ford, the 'Long' appropriately

Pargetting on the Ancient House in Clare

The church and cottages on the green in Cavendish

fine stained glass, depicting friends and relatives of the Clopton family of Kentwell, the clothiers who rebuilt the church.

Melford Hall

Facing the village green is **Melford Hall ❻** (tel: 01787 379 228; www.nationaltrust.org.uk; April–Oct Wed–Sun noon–5pm), a mellow red-brick Tudor mansion with six octagonal turrets. The house was devastated by a fire in 1942 but restored by the Hyde Parker family whose ancestors acquired the house back in 1786. Rooms open to the public include the original banqueting hall, the Regency library and memorabilia of Beatrix Potter, who was related to the family and frequently visited the hall.

Kentwell Hall

At the northern edge of the village and signposted from the green is **Kentwell Hall ❼** (tel: 01787 310 207; www.kentwell.co.uk; house: April–Oct days vary, see website for details, gardens and farm: 11am–5pm, house: noon–4pm), an Elizabethan red-brick manor house. The interior was devastated by fire in the 1820s and was

describing the 2-mile (3km) road running through the village. This wide thoroughfare is lined by delightful 16th-century buildings, a remarkable number of them occupied by antiques shops, art galleries and specialist shops. The Perpendicular **Church of the Holy Trinity**, crowning the hill above the spacious green and seen from afar, is one of the most beautiful in Suffolk. The light-filled nave and chancel have over a hundred windows, and the north aisle has exceptionally

Step back to Tudor England

Kentwell Hall is not just a Tudor house. History here is brought alive by Tudor re-creations, variously featuring medieval pageants, celebrations, activities and everyday life in Tudor times. Special events take place on many weekends throughout the year (see www.kentwell.co.uk for details). Youngsters can also enjoy the Hall grounds and the farm, which was built from scratch in Tudor style for rare-breed farm animals.

Tudor life recreated at Kentwell Hall

Stained glass in the Church of the Holy Trinity, Long Melford

abandoned until the 1970s when the present owners moved in. It has been redeveloped and today is best known for its Tudor or 'Through the Ages' re-creations.

Sudbury

Take the B1064 south for **Sudbury**, a market town on the River Stour best known as the birthplace of Thomas Gainsborough (1727–88), the great English portrait and landscape painter. His bronze statue stands at the top of the market square, and an outstanding collection of his art is on display at **Gainsborough's House** ❽ (46 Gainsborough Street; tel: 01787 372 958; www.gainsborough.org; Mon–Sat 10am–5pm, Sun 11am–5pm), a Georgian building where the artist was born and where he spent his early years. The works on display allow you to explore Gainsborough's whole career, from early portraits and local landscapes to later works from his London period. The exhibition focuses on Gainsborough's life as well as his works of art, with displays of personal memorabilia. The house runs a series of vibrant temporary exhibitions and events throughout the year, and hosts excellent print workshops and summer courses.

Lavenham

From Sudbury the route follows the B1115 and B1071 to **Lavenham** ❾. This is the very finest of the wool towns, preserving an extraordinary number of medieval buildings, many of them half-timbered and tilting at alarming angles. Of the 350 buildings listed as being

A carved wooden pillar on the Guildhall in Lavenham

The Little Hall in Lavenham

has an exhibition on the wool trade and timber-framed buildings, along with an enticing Tudor tea room and garden.

Nearby **Little Hall** (tel: 01787 247 019; www.littlehall.org.uk; April–Oct Tues–Sun 1–4pm, Mon 10am–1pm) is a lovely ochre, half-timbered building owned by the Suffolk Building Preservation Trust. Built in the 14th century for a local family of clothiers, it was enlarged and embellished in Tudor times. The antiques, paintings, china and other objets d'art on view today are the collection of the Gayer Anderson twin brothers, who restored the house in the 1920s.

Harry Potter backdrop

Unsurprisingly, the medieval town of Lavenham has been the backdrop of a number of films and TV series: Stanley Kubrick's *Barry Lyndon*, Michael Reeves' *Witchfinder General*, *Apotheosis 2* with John Lennon and Yoko Ono and the popular early 1990s TV series *Lovejoy*. More recently, in *Harry Potter and the Deathly Hallows*, Lavenham was the location for scenes in Godric's Hollow, birthplace of Harry Potter and his wizarding headmaster, Albus Dumbledore.

of architectural and historical interest, most date from between 1400 and 1500 and the old centre looks much as it did in that era. At one time this was the 14th richest town in Britain, richer than either Lincoln or York, and famous for the blue broadcloth which it exported to Europe. The town is heralded by the magnificent flint tower of the huge late-Perpendicular **Church of St Peter and St Paul**. This was funded primarily by local cloth merchants and the top of the tower carries over 30 coats of arms of the Spring family, the principal wool merchants of Lavenham.

Market place

The stunning **market place** has one of the best examples of half-timbered buildings in the country. The **Guildhall** (tel: 01787 247 646; www.national trust.org.uk; March–Oct daily 11am–5pm, Nov–Feb Fri–Sun 11am–4pm) was the meeting place of the Guild of Corpus Christi, an organization which regulated wool production. Since the decline of the trade, the building has variously served as a prison, workhouse, almshouse, woolstore and, during World War II, a nursery school, restaurant and home for evacuees. It

Kersey

Beautiful old wool towns and villages are two a penny in this region. Tiny Kersey, 9 miles (14km) southeast of Lavenham, oozes charm and was described by the art historian Nikolaus Pevsner as 'the most picturesque village in South Suffolk'. A timeless village of timbered houses and colour-washed cottages, it is set on a steep-sided valley and crowned by the flint tower of its church. Nearby Hadleigh is a market town with some good examples of timber-framed buildings and pargetting.

Eating Out

BURY ST EDMUNDS

Gastrono-me

22 Abbeygate Street; tel: 01284 227 980; www.gastrono-me.co.uk; Mon–Sat 9.30am–5pm.

If it's breakfast you want, this is the place, serving up a fabulous feast until noon. You get everything from granola and pancakes to eggs, bacon and 'posh' baked beans. For lunch there's a wide range of dishes from the UK and beyond. Great value and good fun. £

Maison Bleue

30–1 Churchgate Street; tel: 01284 760 623; www.maisonbleue.co.uk; Tues–Sat noon–2pm and 7–9.30pm.

This is the best place to eat in town: outstanding locally sourced seafood in a charming 17th-century house, with chic contemporary decor. French fine dining is complemented by innovative twists highlighting flavour. Two days' notice (and well-lined pockets) are required for the truly gastronomic *plateau de fruits de mer*. Meat dishes are also served and there are good-value set lunch and dinner menus. £££

BILDESTON

The Bildeston Crown

104 High Street; tel: 01449 740 510; www.thebildestoncrown.com; food: daily noon–2.45pm and 7–9.45pm.

Former coaching inn, now an award-winning hotel, restaurant and bar owned by a Suffolk farmer who produces meat from his own Red Poll herd. Choose from pub classics, house specials or, for the ultimate dining experience, the seven-course tasting menu (for the whole table). Produce, whether it's Sutton Hoo chicken or Suffolk Gold cheese, is locally sourced wherever possible. £££

CAVENDISH

The George

The Green, Peacocks Road; tel: 01787 280 248; www.thecavendishgeorge.co.uk; food: Mon–Sat noon–2pm and 6–9.30pm, Sun noon–3pm.

The George is a charming 16th-century restaurant with rooms in the pretty village of Cavendish, where you'll find a regularly changing menu to complement the seasons, plus produce from the owners' garden. Shell-on smoked prawns with treacle sourdough, followed by pork belly or the daily fish special, finishing with a pecan tart with blood orange salsa. ££

LONG MELFORD

The Black Lion

The Green; tel: 01787 312 356; www.theblacklionlongmelford.com; food: daily 7.30–9.30am, noon–2pm and 7–9pm.

This historic hotel, overlooking the green, lures tourists and locals alike for breakfasts, light lunches, clotted cream teas, full meals and Sunday roasts. Enjoy charred English asparagus in season, rosemary-crusted lamb rump or pan-fried sea bass in a very traditional English setting, with roaring log fires in winter. ££

LAVENHAM

Number Ten

10 Lady Street; tel: 01787 249 438; www.ten-lavenham.co.uk; food: daily noon–2.30pm and 6–9pm.

This wine bar and restaurant is located in a stunning 15th-century building. Its intimate informal ambience has a small but interesting menu to match. Seasonal delights include warm spring onion and stilton tart and fresh local raspberry crème brûlée. Sunday evening is a pizza and pasta menu only. ££

TOUR 10
Cambridge

On this day tour (just under 2 miles/3km), discover the university city and follow on with a leisurely punt along The Backs or upstream to the river village of Grantchester.

In 1209, when riots in Oxford resulted in the hanging of three students, a group of its scholars settled in 'Granta Brygge' and sowed the seeds of England's second university. Prior to its rise as a celebrated seat of learning, it was a small market town on the edge of the swampy fens. The colleges which encroached on the centre were to transform it into a university-dominated town whose intellectual and architectural heritage became the envy of the world. At the same time the pre-eminence of the university gave rise to open conflicts between townspeople and students ('town and gown') which were to flare up on and off for over six centuries.

Today the university comprises 31 independent colleges, with over

Highlights
- King's College
- King's College Chapel
- The Backs
- Trinity College
- St John's College
- Fitzwilliam Museum
- Punting on the Cam

19,500 students. Many visitors see no more than facades, but the true flavour of the colleges can only really be appreciated by penetrating the inner sanctums. Despite the appearance of privacy, the majority of colleges are open to the public and are more approachable than their battlemented gate-towers might suggest. The most famous colleges charge entrance fees and nearly all colleges have restrictions on access, particularly during the exam period (April–June).

Cambridge is also a market town, a shopping centre and the hub of a high-tech revolution. Over 1,500 scientific and technological companies, many based at the burgeoning 'Silicon Valley' on the northern edge of the city, benefit from the research and expertise of the university. A science and technology campus to the west of the city opened in 2013 and the University is currently expanding further to the northwest.

King's College

Start your explorations in the city centre at **King's College ❶**, which was founded in 1441 by Henry VI. It was a grandiose project involving the demolition of a quarter of the medieval centre and causing lasting anger and resentment among the townspeople. This was one of the king's two 'royal and religious' foundations, the other being Eton College, and until 1873 King's College was exclusively for boys from Eton. Work on the famous King's Chapel started in 1446 and took nearly a century to complete.

The breathtaking interior of King's College Chapel

King's College Chapel

Normally there is no public access to the college from the main gateway, and visitors are guided to the north entrance. Facing the college facade, turn right and take Senate House Passage, turning left at the end for **King's College Chapel ❷** (www.kings. cam.ac.uk; term-time: Mon–Fri 9.30am–3.30pm, Sat 9.30am–3.15pm, Sun 1.15–2.30pm, out of term: daily 9.30am–4.30pm, closes 3.30pm Dec–Jan), world-famous for its sublime Gothic architecture and choral music.

Retail therapy

Cambridge has a busy daily market in the centre with books, jewellery and clothes as well as fruit, vegetables and cheese. The Sunday market is strong on arts, crafts and local produce. As well as the high-street names in the award-winning Grand Arcade, the city has a number of interesting, small boutiques. The best hunting grounds are King's Parade, Rose Crescent, Magdalene Street and Bridge Street.

A classic Cambridge satchel in an eye-catching shade of pink

The chapel has the largest fan-vaulted stone ceiling in the world, its only apparent support being the slender columns of the nave. The variety of decoration reflects the changes in style through five reigns and the Wars of the Roses. Dividing the ante-chapel from the choir is the intricately carved dark oak rood screen, a magnificent example of Renaissance woodwork, donated by Henry VIII. The screen bears his initials and those of his Queen, Anne Boleyn, and dates from 1533 (three years before he had her executed). Henry VIII also commissioned the exquisite stained-glass windows on the north, south and east sides of the chapel, depicting scenes from the Old and New Testament (upper and lower levels respectively). The altarpiece is

Rubens' exuberant *Adoration of the Magi*, which was privately donated to the college in 1961.

Henry VI had stipulated that a choir of six men and 16 boy choristers should sing every day in the chapel. Today, the renowned **King's College Choir**, whose Festival of nine Lessons and Carols is broadcast live across the world on Christmas Eve, sings here daily during term time (Mon–Sat 5.30pm, Sun 10.30am and 3.30pm) and visitors are welcome to attend the services.

The Backs

Visitors normally have to leave King's College Chapel by the north gate, but should the main chapel entrance be open take the opportunity to see Great Court and partial views

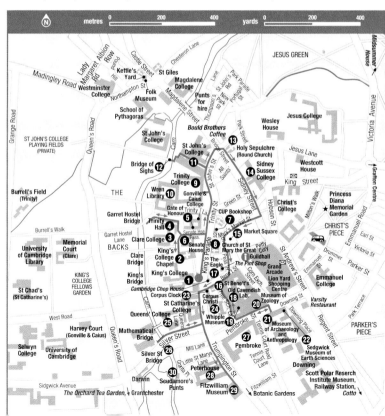

View of 'The Backs'

of '**The Backs**', the glorious lawns, gardens and tree-lined avenues lying between the rear of the colleges and the banks of the Cam. Exiting from the north gate you pass on your left **Clare College** ❸ founded in 1326. The college's Old Court backs onto the River Cam, and Clare Bridge – the oldest of the college bridges – offers picture-postcard views of punts

The Gate of Honour at Gonville and Caius College

drifting past weeping willows, grassy banks and college gardens. For a river view without an admission fee continue along Trinity Lane, passing **Trinity Hall** ❹, one of the smaller, more intimate colleges on the Backs, then left for **Gareth Hostel Bridge**.

Senate House Passage

Retrace your steps to Senate House Passage, stopping at the **Gate of Honour** ❺ of Gonville and Caius College, one of the earliest Renaissance stone structures in the city. Undergraduates of the college pass through the gate to receive their degrees at the graduation ceremonies which take place at the **Senate House** ❻ opposite. Cross Trinity Street for the **Cambridge University Press Bookshop** ❼, the oldest bookshop site in Britain: books have been sold here since 1581.

St Mary the Great

Across the road the **Church of St Mary the Great** ❽ has always been

VIII just before his death in 1546. Trinity has produced 32 Nobel Prize-winners, six British prime ministers, two kings and numerous poets, writers, philosophers and scientists – Francis Bacon, Lord Byron, Ernest Rutherford, Lord Tennyson and Vladimir Nabokov among them. Isaac Newton completed his best-known works here and the apple tree outside the Great Gate, in front of his former study, is said to be descended from the famous tree whose apple dropped on his head and inspired the theory of gravity.

Great Court

The 16th-century **Great Court**, impressive for sheer size and grandeur, with a beautiful carved fountain, is the site of the Great Court Run, where students attempt to run round the perimeter within the time it takes the clock to strike 12 (43 seconds), a scene memorably captured in the 1981 film *Chariots of Fire* (though this was filmed at Eton, not Trinity). The Olympic runner Lord Burghley accomplished the feat in 1927. To the right of King Edward's Tower is the Gothic **chapel**, with imposing statues of celebrated Trinity alumni in the antechapel. The large ivy-clad building on the west range is the Master's Lodge, the Master here being the only one in Cambridge who is nominated by royalty.

an important centre of worship and debate. The great 16th-century Protestant reformers – Erasmus, Cranmer, Latimer and Ridley, who were later burnt at the stake – all preached here. It is worth climbing the 123 steps of the tower for a splendid view of the city below.

Trinity College

Head north along Trinity Street for the Great Gate of **Trinity College ❾** (www.trin.cam.ac.uk; Chapel: daily 10am–5pm), the largest and richest Cambridge college, founded by Henry

Don't walk on the grass

This walk through Cambridge takes about two hours excluding visits to colleges and museums. If the colleges are open to the public (certain times only) it's well worth having a peek. Don't be surprised to see notices forbidding you to walk on the lawns. Only college fellows are permitted to do so.

'Keep off the grass' sign at a Cambridge college

Punting under the Bridge of Sighs

Wren Library

Great Court leads to the cloistered Nevile's Court, flanked on the far side by the **Wren Library** ❿ (www.trin.cam.ac.uk; term-time: Mon–Fri noon–2pm and Sat 10.30am–12.30pm; free), one of the finest classical buildings in the country, designed by Sir Christopher Wren as a gift to the college. The four statues surmounting the library represent the disciplines of Divinity, Law, Physics and Mathematics. The perfectly proportioned interior houses rare manuscripts and first editions, with works by Shakespeare, Milton and Bertrand Russell.

St John's College

Leave Trinity by the Great Gate and turn left for **St John's College** ⓫ (www.joh.cam.ac.uk; daily March–Oct 10am–5pm, Nov–Feb 10am–3.30pm), founded by Lady Margaret Beaufort, mother of Henry VII. The 16th-century Gate Tower is a suitably ornate entrance to a college that is only challenged by Trinity for size and grandeur. Areas accessible to visitors include the very fine Tudor brick First Court,

the grandiose neo-Gothic **chapel**, inspired by Sainte-Chapelle in Paris and designed by George Gilbert Scott in the 1860s, the Tudor brick Second Court and the delicate **Bridge of Sighs** ⓬, a Gothic revival gem modelled on its Venetian namesake. New Court was the first major College building to

The Gate Tower of St John's College

Enjoying an afternoon drink at *The Eagle* pub

be erected west of the river. Known as 'The Wedding Cake', it overlooks the immaculate lawns of The Backs.

The Round Church and Sidney Sussex

Exiting the college by the main entrance, turn left and cross Bridge Street for the 12th-century **Round Church 13**, more formally known as the Church of the Holy Sepulchre. Originally a wayfarers' chapel, it is one of only four surviving Norman round churches in England. A visitor centre with information on the history of Cambridge occupies the interior.

From Bridge Street head towards the centre of town, passing on your left **Sidney Sussex College 14**. One of the smaller colleges, it is notable as the last resting place of the head of Oliver Cromwell. In 1960 the skull (removed from his body almost 300 years earlier) was buried here in the College chapel, but its precise location is a well-kept Cambridge secret. Cromwell had briefly been a student here until his father's death obliged him to return home and take on family responsibilities. In 1643 he returned

as military leader, looted the colleges – which supported King Charles I – and requisitioned their courts as barracks.

Market Square and around

Turn right at the end of Sidney Street for Market Street, leading to the **Market Square 15**. Stalls have been trading at this square since the Middle Ages. It's a lively centre with a general market from Monday to Saturday and an arts, crafts and local produce market on Sundays. Take Peas Hill south of Market Square, to the right of the Guild Hall, and turn right into **Bene't Street**. The Saxon tower of **St Bene't's Church 16** is the city's oldest architectural feature, built in about 1020 during the reign of King Canute. The round holes in the tower are thought to have been made to encourage owls to nest, and catch the mice. Opposite the church is *The Eagle* **17** pub, with plenty of historical interest as well as cask ales.

Science museums

Cambridge has more museums, galleries and collections within a square mile than any other UK city outside London. A cluster of them lie in the centre, though not very

Getting around

Cambridge isn't car friendly. Leave your wheels in one of the five Park and Rides (www.cambridgepark andride.info) and catch the bus into the centre. The city is relatively compact and easy to explore on foot. Alternatively, you could join the students and travel on two wheels. Bikes can be hired from Rutland Cycling (www.rutlandcycling.co.uk) on Corn Exchange Street in the centre. Or join a guided bike tour (www.cambridgebiketours.co.uk).

conspicuously. You won't have time to do them justice on a day trip, but they are all free so you might just want to have a brief look and come back another day. (If not, skip to the Corpus Clock, see below.) Take **Free School Lane** beside St Bene't's Church. Half-way down is the **Old Cavendish Laboratory** ⑱, which became internationally famous for its extraordinary history of discovery and innovation in Physics. It was here that J.J. Thomson discovered the electron (1897), Ernest Rutherford split the atom (1932) and Crick and Watson discovered DNA (1950s). In 1974 the laboratory was moved to a new campus in west Cambridge.

Further down on the left is the **Whipple Museum of the History of Science** ⑲ (tel: 01223 330 906; www.hps.cam.ac.uk/whipple; Mon–Fri 12.30–4.30pm; free) with a fascinating array of scientific instruments dating from the Middle Ages to the present day. Turn left at the end of the lane for Downing Street. On the

left, the **Museum of Zoology** ⑳ (www.museum.zoo.cam.ac.uk; free) includes specimens discovered by Charles Darwin on his 1831 voyage on the *Beagle*.

Over the road the **Museum of Archaeology and Anthropology** ㉑ (tel: 01223 333 516; www.maa.cam. ac.uk; Tues–Sat 10.30am–4.30pm, Sun noon–4.30pm; free) displays art and culture from around the world and includes a 45ft (14-metre) totem pole and Pacific material collected on Captain Cook's voyages.

Tucked away on the same site is the **Sedgwick Museum of Earth Sciences** ㉒ (tel: 01223 333 456; www.sedgwickmuseum.org; Mon–Fri 10am–1pm and 2–5pm, Sat 10am–4pm; free), housing Britain's oldest intact geological collection including a 125,000-year-old hippo found locally, marine reptiles, dinosaurs and an exhibition on 'Darwin the Geologist'.

The Corpus Clock

Return to King's Parade, on the corner with Bene't Street, where tourists are normally mingling around the **Corpus Clock** ㉓ on Corpus Christi's

The Corpus Clock

The Mathematical Bridge

Taylor Library. This 24-carat gold-plated stainless steel disc has a large, grim-looking grasshopper perched on top which 'devours time' in front of your eyes. The clock has no hands or numerals, but there are 60 slots cut into its face which light up to show the time. The £1m time-eater was unveiled in 2008 by famous Cambridge physicist, Stephen Hawking. It was a radical idea, especially for a college whose Old Court resisted 18th-century refurbishment and is the oldest surviving enclosed court in Cambridge. For the main entrance of **Corpus Christi College** ㉔, turn left along Trumpington Street. Old Court to the left dates from 1352 and gives you an insight into the secluded and private atmosphere which characterized the early University.

Queens' College

Take the next turn right, Silver Street, passing on the right **Queens' College** ㉕ (www.queens.cam.ac.uk; most days 10am–4.30pm, except during exams, check website for details). The Cam divides the college in two and is spanned by the **Mathematical Bridge**. Contrary to popular belief, this was not designed by Newton, nor was it built without the use of bolts. It was in fact constructed in 1904 as an identical replacement of the original (1749) using bolts at the main joints. The College's Old Court is one of the finest examples of a medieval quadrangle, and, beyond the passage lies the enchanting Cloister Court, flanked by the half-timbered President's Lodge.

The Eagle's DNA

It was in *The Eagle* on Bene't Street in 1953 that Watson and Crick announced to the world that they had discovered 'the secret of life' (DNA). A plaque in this old coaching inn records the event, and the pub serves 'Eagle's DNA ale' to commemorate the discovery. Check out too the ceiling of the RAF Bar, covered with the names of British and American RAF pilots returning from World War II, signed with cigarette lighters and candle-smoke.

From **Silver Street Bridge** ❷⓺ you can see **Scudamore's** (see page 95), pioneers of punt hire, who have been in the business for over 100 years.

Pembroke and Peterhouse

Return to Trumpington Street and turn right. The college on the left is **Pembroke** ❷⓻, best known for its chapel (1663–5), the first work to be completed by Sir Christopher Wren. William Pitt the Younger (1759–1806), a precocious student, came up to Pembroke at the age of 14, and became Britain's youngest prime minister only 10 years later. Further down, on the right, is **Peterhouse** ❷⓼, the oldest of the colleges, founded in 1284 by the Bishop of Ely. Sir Frank Whittle, inventor of the jet engine, was a student here, as was Charles Babbage, whose work led to the modern computer.

The Fitzwilliam Museum

Beyond Peterhouse you're unlikely to miss the formidable neoclassical facade of the **Fitzwilliam Museum** ❷⓽ (tel: 01223 332 900; www.fitzmuseum.

cam.ac.uk; Tues–Sat 10am–5pm, Sun noon–5pm; free), one of the great treasure houses of Britain. The museum is a mini-Louvre, with almost half a million works of art from around the world. The nucleus is a priceless collection of paintings, books and manuscripts belonging to the museum's founder, Viscount Fitzwilliam. The Fitzwilliam was one of Britain's earliest public picture galleries and its internationally famous collection includes masterpieces by Italian Renaissance artists, Flemish masters and French Impressionists. There are Egyptian, Greek, Roman and West Asiatic antiquities, glass, sculpture and armour, as well as outstanding displays of ceramics, illuminated musical and literary manuscripts and a fascinating collection of fans. When it comes to a break from sightseeing there is an excellent shop with cards, books and gifts, plus an adjoining café.

Punting on the Cam

One of the most enduring images of Cambridge is of languid summers

Paintings at the Fitzwilliam Museum

Punters on the Cam

spent punting along on the river. The calm and shallow waters of the River Cam are ideally suited to the flat-bottomed punts, which are propelled by pushing a long pole against the riverbed. Pleasure punts were introduced in Edwardian times; before that they were used by fishermen and reed cutters in the Fens. As ever, the two major university cities have their own approaches: in Cambridge, the tradition is for the punter to stand on the boat's short deck (known as the 'counter' or 'till'), whereas in Oxford, you stand at the other end, with the till at the front.

Punts can be hired at the bottom of Mill Lane at **Scudamore's** ❸ (tel: 01223 359 750; www.scudamores. com; punt chauffeurs available). Most visitors choose to glide along The Backs behind Trinity, King's and several other colleges – though this stretch of river does become congested in summer. With time on your hands

Kettle's Yard

On Northampton Street, north of the city centre, Kettle's Yard (www.kettlesyard.co.uk; free) is a fascinating gallery in four cottages, which Tate Gallery curator Jim Ede restored and made into his home in the 1950s. He filled this haven of peace with works by Ben Nicholson, Henry Moore and many other leading artists. A major development over several years has seen a new education wing and café added, plus improved exhibition galleries, while leaving the house untouched.

Kettle's Yard

The Botanic Garden

A must for any garden lover, the Botanic Garden (www.botanic.cam.ac.uk) is a 40-acre (16-hectare) oasis providing year-round colour and structure: 8,000 plants species, a magnificent tree collection, glasshouses of tropical plants, a Scented Garden, a Winter Garden and a Genetics Garden which illustrates how genetic variation plays on the appearance of plants. It's a reminder that the garden was established by Professor Henslow, the tutor who inspired Charles Darwin.

One of the glasshouses in the Botanic Garden

you could take the more tranquil route through the lush meadows to Grantchester. A skilled punter should be able to reach the village in 1.5 hours or less.

Rupert Brooke's Grantchester

The riverside village of Grantchester was immortalized by Rupert Brooke, the poet who wrote movingly of the futility of war and died in World War I at the age of 28. A student of King's College, Brooke spent much of his time here, studying, swimming, walking barefoot and boating to Cambridge. The last two lines of his eulogy, 'The Old Vicarage, Grantchester', written in nostalgic mood from a Berlin café, still reverberate in the village lanes:

Stands the Church clock at ten to three
And is there honey still for tea?

It is believed the clock had broken in Brooke's day – if this was not the case it was altered to stand at ten to three for several years as a memorial to the poet. The clock today is fully functional but there is still honey for tea beneath the apple trees in *The Orchard Tea Garden* (see page 97).

During the pre-war period, The Orchard was a favourite haunt of Brooke and a group of friends, who became known as the Grantchester Group or the 'neo-pagans': the philosophers, Bertrand Russell and Ludwig Wittgenstein, the writers, E.M. Forster and Virginia Woolf, the economist, Maynard Keynes and the artist, Augustus John. Brooke lodged at Orchard House in 1909, then later moved to the old Vicarage next door, which is now home of novelist and former politician, Jeffrey Archer. Brooke, who was buried in an olive grove on the island of Skiros in Greece, is commemorated on a war memorial in the churchyard, along with other war victims.

Rupert Brooke statue in Grantchester

Eating Out

Bould Brothers Coffee

16 Round Church Street; tel: 07796 320 049; www.bouldbrotherscoffee.co.uk; Mon–Fri 8am–6pm, Sat 9am–6pm, Sun 10am–5pm.

Locals are billing this as some of the best coffee in town. Brothers Max and Alex Bould bring experience and passion to their coffee making, complemented by great snacks – home-made banana bread, toasted brioche and delicious pastries. Range of loose leaf teas too. £

Cambridge Chop House

1 King's Parade; tel: 01223 359 506; www.cambscuisine.com; Mon–Thurs noon–10.30pm, Fri & Sat until 11pm, Sun until 9.30pm, also breakfast daily 9–11am.

Right in the centre, the Chop House serves no-nonsense British classics – 'the sort of food your grandmother may have cooked' – accompanied by Cambridge real ales from the cask and wines from Languedoc-Roussillon. ££

Cotto

Gonville Hotel, Gonville Place; tel: 01223 302 010; www.cottocambridge. co.uk; Tues–Sat 6.30–11.30pm.

This Cambridge favourite is a top dining choice for locals. Chef Hans Schweitzer has worked in top-notch restaurants and his modern European dishes rarely disappoint. £££

Midsummer House

Midsummer Common; tel: 01223 369 299; www.midsummerhouse. co.uk; Wed–Sat noon–1.30pm, Tues–Thurs also 7–8.30pm, Fri & Sat also 6.30–9.30pm.

Chef Daniel Clifford serves elegant, modern European cuisine in the stylish surroundings of a Victorian house on the banks of the Cam. The food is seriously sophisticated, with occasional unexpected textures and combinations. This is the only Michelin two-star restaurant in East Anglia, with prices to match. £££

The Orchard Tea Garden

47 Mill Way, Grantchester; tel: 01223 840 230; www.theorchardteagarden. co.uk; daily April–Oct 9am–6pm, Nov–Feb 9.30am–5pm (until 6pm Sat–Sun).

An oasis of thought-provoking calm that became the haunt of Rupert Brooke and a remarkable group of his friends. A pamphlet lists famous people who have taken tea here, among them Bertrand Russell, E.M. Forster, Virginia Woolf, Maynard Keynes, along with royalty and 21st-century celebrities. The current management aims to continue the traditional nature of the establishment. Coffee, teas and light lunches, inside or out. £

The Pint Shop

10 Pea's Hill; tel: 01223 981 070; www.pintshop.co.uk; food: daily noon–10pm (Sat & Sun opens 11am). This pub and restaurant has become a hit for its beers, no-frills menu and great bar snacks. It offers around 16 types of beers and some 100 gins along with Welsh rarebit, filled brioche buns and Scotch eggs or delicious main meat dishes cooked over charcoal. The setting is simple but welcoming. ££

Varsity Restaurant

35 St Andrews Street; tel: 01223 356 060; www.varsityrestaurant. co.uk; Mon–Thurs noon–3pm and 5.30–10pm, Fri & Sat noon–10.30pm and Sun noon–9.30pm.

This is Cambridge's oldest restaurant with a modern twist. Choose stuffed smoked aubergine and hake fillet from the lunch menu or opt for the a la carte menu which serves tasty mains from tuna steak to pigeon breast. ££

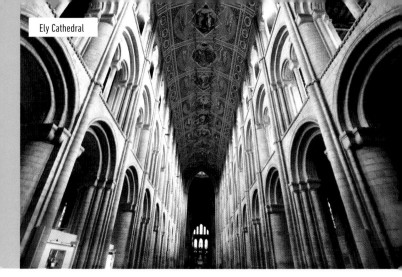

Ely Cathedral

TOUR 11

Around Cambridge

See the high spots around Cambridge on this day tour:
Ely Cathedral, the famous horseracing centre of Newmarket and
the beautiful market town of Saffron Walden.

Derived from the Saxon *elge*, or
eel district, Ely was formerly an
inaccessible island, surrounded by
marshland which seethed with eels.
Following the draining of the Fenland
in the 17th century, the settlement
developed into a thriving market town.
Today it is a prosperous little city,
completely dominated by its famous
cathedral. It lies 16 miles (25km)
north of Cambridge on the A10.

Ely Cathedral

Rising ship-like above the city and
surrounding fenland is the magnificent
Norman **Cathedral of Ely** ❶ (tel:
01353 667 735; www.elycathedral.org;
daily 7am–6.30pm, Sun until 5.30pm
in winter). St Ethelreda selected this
site for a Benedictine monastery for

Highlights

- Ely Cathedral
- Palace House, Newmarket
- National Stud
- Saffron Walden
- Audley End

monks and nuns in AD 673. The
building you see today was begun in
1083, around the time that Hereward
the Wake famously used Ely as a refuge
when being pursued by William the
Conqueror. Eventually the monks tired
of the siege and showed the conqueror's
men the secret pathway through the
marshes, giving Hereward away.

Inside the cathedral the sheer size
takes your breath away – the nave

The Stained Glass Museum

Follow the eel

Ely's eel trail is a circular way-marked walk which follows the life cycle of an eel through five works of art. The heritage trail starts at the tourist office, former home of Oliver Cromwell, then takes in the Waterside, a great spot for a boat trip, riverside walk or cream tea. Eel-themed artworks include a 9-metre (30ft) long willow eel hive, the traditional means of eel-fishing on the River Ouse.

is one of the longest in Britain. The crowning glory is the **timber octagon** – an octagonal tower of wood and glass built high on the back of the nave in an extraordinary feat of engineering. In the evening the lantern reflects the rays of the dying sun; by night its glass gleams, illuminated by a light within. For the best views, join one of the guided tours (10.45am, noon, 2pm, 3pm, also 1pm July & Aug), which take you to the top of the Octagon (170 steps) and also up the **West Tower** (288 steps) with great views of the Fens. The **Lady Chapel**, the largest of its kind in the country, formerly glowed with medieval stained-glass windows, but these, along with heads of the statuettes, were destroyed during the Reformation. The **Stained Glass Museum** (www.stainedglassmuseum.com) traces the history of stained glass from 1200 to the present day and demonstrates glass-making techniques.

Newmarket

Return to the A10, turn left on to the A1123, passing **Wicken Fen** (see page 100), then right when you reach the A142 for **Newmarket** ❷. Racing here dates back to 1174, but its popularity as a horseracing centre grew when

Charles I, who inaugurated the first cup race in 1634, firmly established it as the 'sport of kings'. Newmarket became the most fashionable race course in the country. Today nearly 3,000 horses, including some of the country's most thoroughbred studs, are trained on Newmarket Heath. There are two magnificent race courses, the Rowley Mile, named after Charles II's favourite horse 'Old Rowley' and

Wicken Fen

Nine miles south of Ely, Wicken Fen (Lode Lane, Wicken, tel: 01353 720 274; www.nationaltrust.org.uk; daily dawn–dusk; facilities open at 10am) is Britain's oldest nature reserve and gives you a good idea of what the Fens would have looked like before their reclamation. The site spreads over 700 acres (280 hectares), and is home to rare species of plants, insects and birds. The site has nature trails, bird hides, boat trips and cycles for hire. There is also a dragonfly centre and an old Fenland thatched cottage.

Golden dragonfly at Wicken Fen Nature Reserve

Saffron Walden

For **Saffron Walden** ❹, follow the B1061 and B1052. The town gets its name from the orange crocus dye that made it wealthy – formerly it was called Chipping Walden. Today it is a prosperous and delightfully unspoilt market town with timber-framed buildings and fine examples of pargetting, or decorative moulded plasterwork. The **Church of St Mary**, whose lofty spire can be spotted from almost anywhere in town, is the largest parish church in Essex and a fine example of the Perpendicular style. A market (Tues and Sat) has been held here since 1141 and shoppers can also enjoy the many independent little shops.

the July Race Course. On a weekday morning in Newmarket you can watch the racehorses training on The Gallops, the heath east of the town. There are five classic flat races every year (see www.thejockeyclub.co.uk for details).

Located in Palace Street is **Palace House** (tel: 01638 667 314; www.palacehousenewmarket. co.uk; daily 10am–5pm), home to the National Heritage Centre for Horse Racing and Sporting Art, opened by the Queen in 2016. In this fabulous centre you can visit the National Horseracing Museum, try out a racehorse simulator, meet retired racehorses in Rothschild Yard and see daily demonstrations as well. The galleries include some fine works by the most famous of horse artists, George Stubbs. The **National Stud** ❸ (www.nationalstud.co.uk; tours only, Feb–Sept Wed–Sun 11.15am, March–Sept also Sat & Sun 2pm, Oct Fri–Sun 11.15am; booking essential) lies 2 miles (3km) southwest of the centre, next to the July Race Course. This is the only commercial thoroughbred stud farm in the UK that allows the public to see behind the scenes.

Audley End House

Audley End House

About 1 mile (1.6km) west of Saffron Walden is **Audley End House ❺** (tel: 01799 522 842; www.english-heritage. org.uk; house: April–Sept daily noon–5pm, Oct noon–4pm, gardens, stables and service wing: daily April–Sept 10am–6pm, Oct 10am–5pm, Nov–March Sat & Sun 10am–4pm), a grandiose Jacobean mansion set amid magnificent parkland designed by Capability Brown. The biggest house in England at the time (now half the size that it used to be), it takes its name from Sir Thomas Audley, Henry VIII's Lord Chancellor, who adapted the buildings of Walden Abbey. His grandson, Thomas Howard, Lord Treasurer to James I, turned it into a lavish mansion where he entertained the king. The 18th century saw grand changes under architects Sir John Vanbrugh and Robert Adam. But the original facade has been retained and the Great Hall preserves its huge, elaborately carved Jacobean oak screen and hammerbeam roof. Many of the state apartments have been restored to their former splendour. The service wing gives a fascinating insight into life 'below stairs' in Victorian times. In the grounds children can meet the horses, let off steam in the outdoor play area or take a trip on the miniature railway (April–Oct Sat & Sun, daily during summer school holidays).

Return to Cambridge on the M11 via Duxford, home to the **Imperial War Museum ❻** (tel: 01223 835 000; www.iwm.org.uk). Save this for another time; it could occupy an entire day!

Eating Out

ELY
The Old Fire Engine House
25 St Mary's Street; tel: 01353 662 582; www.theoldfireenginehouse. co.uk; daily 12.15–2pm, 3.30–5.15pm and 7–9pm, closed Sun eve.
In the shadow of Ely Cathedral, this charming Georgian house has a walled garden and a farmhouse ambience. Food is wholesome British, with seasonal local ingredients and Fenland recipes. Everything is cooked to order whether it is venison from the Denham estate, steak and kidney pie or home-cooked ham and piccalilli. Service is attentive and second helpings are usually on offer! Scrumptious cream teas too. ££

SUTTON
EBB & Flow Sutton
59–61 High Street; tel: 02087 707 337; www.ebbflowsutton.co.uk; food: Mon–Sun noon–9pm.
Laidback venue which serves classic pub grub from fish and chips to a range of burgers. The Dirty Chilli Cheeseburger is an epic feast. For pudding think a towering ice cream sundae and an oozing salted caramel ice cream cheesecake sandwich. Vegan and vegetarian options are also available, along with a kids' menu. There is plenty of outdoor seating, too. ££

ARKESDEN
The Axe and Compasses
The High Street; tel: 01799 550 272; www.axeandcompasses.co.uk; food: Mon–Sat noon–2pm and 6.30–9pm, Sun noon–2.15pm.
This traditional village pub, with thatched roof, beamed restaurant and plenty of atmosphere, is one of the most popular in the area. Food is mainly traditional British, with an emphasis on beef and fish, which comes direct from Billingsgate Market. Desserts are to die for. Traditional three-course set lunch is served on Sundays. ££

ART AND ARTISTS

For centuries artists have taken inspiration from the Suffolk and Norfolk scenery, from the great 19th-century landscape artist, John Constable, to modern sculptor Maggi Hambling.

John Constable was born in East Bergholt and even when he moved to London, he would journey home frequently to sketch the valley of the Stour. 'I associate my careless boyhood with all that lies on the Banks of the Stour; those scenes made me a painter, and I am grateful'. The famous *Hay Wain* failed to receive much acclaim when exhibited in London but at the Paris Salon three years later it created a sensation. The painting had a huge influence on the development of landscape painting, especially on the French Impressionists.

Thomas Gainsborough, the great English painter of portraits and landscapes, was born in Sudbury in 1727 and most of his early work was local Suffolk scenes. Although he made his living as a painter of portraits of the aristocracy and royal family, his first love was always landscape.

Sir Alfred Munnings (1878–1959) was primarily an equestrian painter

Reflection of Willy Lott's House, Flatford

The Norwich School

Founded in 1803, the Norwich School was a group of landscape artists who painted local scenes directly from nature, rather than the traditional imaginary or idealized landscapes. The leading lights were John Crome, who was self-taught and influenced by the 17th-century Dutch school and the more prolific John Sell Cotman, best known for his watercolours.

Where to see art

Gainsborough's House, Sudbury (www.gainsborough.org). Birthplace of Thomas Gainsborough, displaying a large collection of his works.
The Munnings Art Museum, Dedham (www.munningsmuseum.org.uk). Home of the equine-painter, Sir Alfred Munnings.
Christchurch Mansion, Ipswich (www.cimuseums.org.uk). The largest collection of Constable's and Gainsborough's work outside London.
Norwich Castle Museum and Art Gallery (www.museums.norfolk.gov.uk). The most comprehensive collection of the work of the Norwich School, covering three generations and some 50 artists.
Fitzwilliam Museum, Cambridge (www.fitzmuseum.cam.ac.uk). Works by Constable, Gainsborough, the Norwich School and Maggi Hambling.
Aldeburgh: Maggi Hambling's *Scallop* (see page 68). Aldeburgh also has some notable galleries, including Caroline Wiseman Modern and Contemporary on Crag Path.
Flatford Mill: Visit the exact spot where the artist painted *The Hay Wain* (now in the National Gallery, London).

who lived in Dedham for much of his life, but he was also a portraitist and landscape artist – as you can see from the works of art in his house in Dedham, now a museum.

Walberswick

The Suffolk village of Walberswick has always been a favourite for artists and today has a thriving arts community. Philip Wilson Steer, the progressive British painter who looked to France for inspiration, produced seascapes of Walberswick which are regarded as some of the finest Impressionist works by an English artist. The painter rented his house next to the *Bell Inn* to the Scottish architect and artist, Charles Rennie Mackintosh, who painted botanical sketches around Walberswick.

Boats on the River
Stour in Flatford

TOUR 12

Colchester and Constable Country

This half-day, 15-mile (24km) tour takes in the oldest
recorded town in Britain and the tranquil Stour Valley,
which inspired the great landscape painter John Constable.

Colchester owes its rich history to its
setting on the River Colne, 8 miles
(13km) from the sea. Known as
Camulodunum (fortress of the Celtic
war god, Camulos), it became the
first capital of Roman Britain, when
London was just a trading post. Queen
Boudicca of the Iceni tribe razed the
Roman town to the ground in AD
60, before going on to do likewise in
London and St Albans. The Romans
rebuilt it, this time erecting a 10ft
(3-metre) thick defensive wall around
the city. A long section of this original
town wall and the Roman gateway still
stand, but the main historic attraction
is the castle.

Use either the Priory Street or
Nunns Road car park for easiest access
to the castle.

Highlights

- Colchester Castle
- Dedham Village
- Flatford Mill
- Bridge Cottage

Colchester Castle

William the Conqueror built the
Norman castle on the ruins of the
Roman Temple of Claudius. The
Norman Keep, the largest in Britain,
survives from the mighty fortress, and
is home to the **Castle Museum**
❶ (High Street; tel: 01206 282 939;
www.cimuseums.org.uk; Mon–Sat
10am–5pm, Sun 11am–5pm). The
sheer scale of the walls is impressive,
and the museum within them packs

in a huge amount of information on the history of the city, from prehistory to the Civil War. After a £4-million revamp, it has a host of interactive displays, 3D animations and numerous family activities – alongside the most important Roman British collection outside London. Displays include exquisite Roman pottery, glass, jewellery, statues and mosaics. The Colchester Vase, discovered in a grave in Colchester and decorated with four gladiators and a hunting scene, is the most famous pot from Roman Britain. The Roman vaults and the rooftop can be viewed as part of a behind-the-scenes guided tour.

Display at the Castle Museum in Colchester

Castle Park

The castle forms part of **Castle Park** (daily 7.30am until dusk; free), a green oasis in the heart of the city, landscaped in the Victorian era but formerly used by farmers for grazing their sheep and cloth-makers from the Dutch Quarter for drying out their textiles. A large expanse of parkland, it has a boating pond, crazy golf and putting green, adventure playground and Victorian bandstand with music most Sundays in summer. In summer it sees open air-concerts and festivals; and it's a great spot for a picnic.

At the entrance to Castle Park is the **Hollytrees Museum** (www.ci museums.org.uk; Mon–Sat 10am–5pm; free). This handsome Georgian house (which doubles up as the Visitor Information Centre) is a museum of domestic life and childhood, full of fascinating toys, costumes and decorative arts. The approach is very much a hands-on one, aimed at families. The huge dolls house is particularly popular.

Dutch Quarter

In the 16th century, Flemish weavers settled in Colchester to boost the textile trade and the town became an important weaving centre. The gabled and timber-framed houses of the peaceful **Dutch quarter** can be seen in Maidenburgh Street, bordering Castle Park behind the castle (easy access from Nunns Road car park). This is one of the few old quarters to survive. Colchester has seen a large amount of modern development over the years, inevitably controversial in a city so

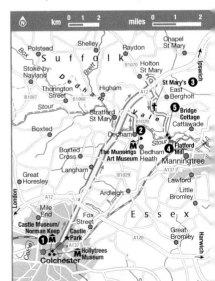

Boudicca

Boudicca was married to Prasutagus, King of the of the Iceni tribe, who had a favoured position with the Romans and was allowed to rule independently. But when Prasutagus died the Romans turned on the Iceni, allegedly flogging Boudicca and raping her daughters. In AD 60 the flame-haired Iceni warrior led a fierce revolt, torching the three main Roman strongholds of the south, Colchester, London and St Albans. The rebellion was quashed within a year and Boudicca is believed to have taken poison to avoid capture by the Romans.

steeped in history. The best way to see its surviving historic monuments, including the oldest surviving Roman gateway in Britain, is to follow the Heritage Trail (booklet from tourist office in Hollytrees, £2.50), a circular walk starting at the castle.

Dedham

From Colchester follow signs for the A12 to Ipswich, which you join 2 miles (3km) north of the city. Take the B1029 exit and follow signs for **Dedham ❷**. If there are no parking spaces along the main street – often the case in this popular village – follow the signs to the car park near the river. Constable used to walk daily across the River Stour from his home in East Bergholt to the grammar school in Dedham. Today it is a prosperous, quintessentially English village, the High Street lined by immaculately preserved medieval and Georgian houses, interspersed by cafés and pubs to tempt even the most discerning of palates. The village grew rich on the wool industry, proof of which can be seen in the Marlborough Head, where the original heavy beams and massive hook used to weigh the heavy fleeces and sacks of wool.

The **Church of St Mary**, which was built in 1492–1520 with profits from the wool trade, features in several of Constable's paintings. Tom Keating, the famous art forger and art restorer, who copied some of Constable's paintings, is buried in the churchyard. Further down the High Street, the United Reform church is home to the **Dedham Arts and Crafts Centre**, with a wide selection of local and other works of art and a good café.

The Munnings Art Museum (Castle House; tel: 01206 322 127; www.munningsmuseum.org.uk; April–Oct Wed–Sun 2–5pm, café open from 10am), a mile (1.5km) further along the street, was home of horse-painter Sir Alfred Munnings, and has a collection of his paintings. It can also be reached via a footpath beside St Mary's Church (allow 15 minutes).

The Church of St Mary in Dedham

Shoppers at the Dedham Arts and Crafts Centre

Dedham Vale

A source of inspiration to Constable and other well-known British artists, the tranquil **Dedham Vale** on the Suffolk-Essex border is a protected area of gently rolling fields, wooded valleys and a meandering river. From the Dedham Boathouse you can hire rowing boats, following the river as it winds through the water meadows to Flatford, or take the *Stour Trusty II*, a little electric boat, (www.riverstourtrust.org; certain days only April to October); alternatively, the 1.5-mile (2.5km) footpath follows the natural line of the River Stour along pretty water meadows. By car it's a longer, circuitous route of 5.5 miles (9km).

East Bergholt

Follow the B1029 and turn left under the A12 at the Church of Stratford St Mary. Turn left again, signposted to Flatford, to join the A12. The road to **East Bergholt** (B1070) is marked off the A12. Turn right at *The Carriers Arms* pub. A plaque on the black railings between the church and the village shop marks the site of Constable's childhood home – this disappeared long ago. The parish **Church of St Mary** ❸ has the graves of Constable's parents and Willy Lot, whose cottage he painted. Inside, a narrow, unremarkable panel at the foot of the first stained glass window on the right commemorates the artist and his wife. The large wooden cage in the churchyard houses the heaviest bells currently rung in England. The church bell tower was begun in 1525 but work ceased through lack of funds and the cage was built as a temporary protection for the bells.

Beth Chatto Gardens

For gardening enthusiasts there are two real gems in the region. The first is Beth Chatto Gardens at Elmstead Market (www.bethchatto.co.uk). With her garden writing and her stunning woodland, water and gravel gardens, Beth Chatto has captivated the horticultural world for over 50 years. The Place for Plants, East Bergholt (www.placeforplants.co.uk) is a family-run garden, arboretum and plant centre, with a wonderful walled garden and a great choice of plants.

A common oak tree at The Place for Plants

John Constable

Constable's most famous painting, *The Hay Wain*, painted at Flatford Mill, was singled out for a gold medal by the French King Charles X, in the Paris Salon of 1824. At the time Constable's reputation was considerably higher in France than it was in England. He was not elected to the Royal Academy in London until the age of 53 (Turner was admitted at 25).

Constable's *The Hay Wain*

It has remained in the churchyard ever since and its bells are rung every Sunday.

Flatford

Continue past the church and follow signs for **Flatford**. From the car park (free to National Trust members) a path leads down to the River Stour. A Visitor Centre provides information on the various footpaths, including nature trails for children and riverside walks to Dedham or RSPB Cattawade Marshes.

From an early age Constable captured his rural homeland on canvas and several of his greatest works of art depict scenes which lay within a few hundred yards of his home. It is well worth taking a short guided walk (three or four a day in summer, call ahead 01206 297 201) showing you the famous scenes that he painted, comparing what you see now with reproductions of his paintings. The picturesque **Flatford Mill** ❹, best viewed from across the water, and Willy Lott's House (on the near side of the river) are both recognisable subjects of *The Hay Wain*, painted in 1821. Constable's father was a prosperous merchant who owned Flatford Mill, along with Dedham Mill, and a house, garden and windmill in East Bergholt.

Although most of the buildings are closed to the public (they are run by the National Trust and leased out to the Field Studies Council for art and environmental courses), it's a lovely spot for walking or hiring a rowing boat. But do be aware of crowds at weekends or Bank Holidays in high season.

Bridge Cottage

The charming thatched **Bridge Cottage** ❺ (www.nationaltrust. org.uk; check website for opening times; free) lies just upstream from

Willy Lott's House at Flatford Mill

Flatford Mill. The cottage displays reproductions of Constable's paintings of views in the area, alongside relevant quotes from his correspondence.

But most visitors soon end up in the National Trust gift shop and café for riverside cream teas, beside the dry dock where barges, known as 'lighters', were built and repaired. Seeing the river today, it is hard to believe it was formerly a busy waterway, used by the barges to transport coal, bricks, lime and corn.

Opposite the cottage is the pretty **RSPB Flatford Wildlife Garden** (April–Oct daily 10.30am–4.30pm; free), with flower borders, a small meadow, woodland gardens and a kitchen garden – all designed with wildlife in mind. Activities like pond-dipping and mini-beast hunting are held here in the holidays.

Eating Out

COLCHESTER

Bellapais Steakhouse & Greek Restaurant

St John's Street; tel: 01206 571 830; www.bella-pais.co.uk; Tues–Fri 6–10pm, Sat 5–10.30pm, Sun 5–9.30pm.

This family-run restaurant has been serving up delicious Greek and Cypriot dishes for the last 30 years. It's a haven for meat eaters with plenty of kebabs and steaks on offer. The vegetarian moussaka is a firm favourite, too. Generous-sized meze dishes are also available. ££

DEDHAM

Boathouse Restaurant

Mill Lane; tel: 01206 323 153; www.dedhamboathouse.com; Tues–Sat noon–2.30pm and 6.30–9.30pm, Sun noon–2.30pm.

Overlooking the tranquil River Stour, the varied menu at the Boathouse features several meat dishes, a 'catch of the day' fish dish and vegetarian meals such as Thai curry or risotto. Summer specials, a seasonal 'row and dine' set menu and good-value tasting menu in the winter months. ££

Le Talbooth

Gunhill, signposted off the A12; tel: 01206 323 150; www.milsomhotels.com/le-talbooth; Mon–Sat noon–2.30pm and 7–9.30pm, Sun noon–2.30pm.

Save this one for a special occasion. Part of the upmarket Milsom Hotels and Restaurants, Le Talbooth is a luxurious and beautifully located restaurant in a half-timbered house on the banks of the Stour. You'll find impeccable service and treats such as Dedham Vale beef fillet. £££

EAST BERGHOLT

The Carriers Arms

Heath Road; tel: 01206 298 392; www.thecarriersarms.co.uk; food: Mon–Sat noon–2.15pm and 6–8.45pm, Sun noon–7.30pm.

This friendly traditional family-run pub is in the heart of the village and popular with locals and visitors alike. There's a good pub-grub menu with staples such as fish pie and lasagne alongside more spicy dishes such as sweet chili prawn stir fry and lamb rogan josh. £

STRATFORD ST MARY

Hall Farm

Church Road; tel: 01206 323 600; www.hallfarmshop.com; Mon–Sat 9am–5pm, Sun 10am–4pm.

Come for breakfast, coffee and home-made cake or a leisurely lunch at this lovely family-run café-cum-deli-cum-gift shop. The deli has a great selection and is ideal for a picnic. Menus often feature prize-winning beef and lamb from the farm; bread, scones and cakes are baked daily. ££

Go Ape! at High Lodge, Thetford Forest

Norfolk Coast Path sign

TRIP TIPS
Active Pursuits

From cycling and swimming to fishing and golf, the region has a host of activities to keep you occupied.

Walking

Thanks to the easy-going gently undulating landscapes and variety of wildlife, the region is ideal for walking. Tourist information offices and visitor centres at nature reserves provide leaflets on local footpaths (often chargeable) of varying lengths. The Ordnance Survey maps, either the Explorer or Landranger series, mark footpaths and are invaluable for walkers.

Several long-distance footpaths cross the region. One of the best known is the 46-mile (74km) Peddars Way, from Knettishall Heath Country Park in Suffolk to Holme-next-the-Sea on the Norfolk coast. This joins the Norfolk Coast Path which runs from Hunstanton to Sea Palling, covering some 63 miles (101km) and taking in salt marshes, working fishing harbours and miles of sand dunes. The best way to explore a section of the footpath is to take a one-way walk and use the Coasthopper bus (tel: 01553 776 980; www.coasthopper.co.uk; see page 122) to return to your starting point. The Weaver's Way (60 miles/96km) from Cromer to Great Yarmouth takes in some of the best Norfolk Broads scenery and links with the Wherryman's Way (35 miles/56km), which connects Great Yarmouth with Norwich, mainly along the riverside. The Suffolk Coast Path (52 miles/ 83km) from Felixstowe in the south up the coast to Southwold takes in an Area of Outstanding Natural Beauty.

Cycling

With physically undemanding terrain and abundant cycle paths, both Norfolk and Suffolk are popular with cyclists. Tourist information centres offer a comprehensive selection of cycle leaflets and maps, many of them downloadable. The Norfolk Coast Cycleway goes all the way from King's Lynn to Great Yarmouth, and is part of the Sustrans National Cycle Network (tel: 0117 926 8893; www.sustrans. org.uk). Some of Suffolk's prettiest countryside is covered by three lovely routes – Suffolk Coastal, Heart of Suffolk and South Suffolk – designed for leisure cyclists and using quiet lanes (www.discoversuffolk.org.uk). The routes are clearly signposted all the way so you're unlikely to get lost. The Painter's Trail is a 69-mile (110km) route exploring the locations painted by the famous East Anglian landscape painters, which can be broken down into shorter stages. For well-organized cycling holidays in Norfolk and Suffolk contact Cycle Breaks (tel: 01449 721 555; www.cyclebreaks.co.uk). High Lodge, Thetford Forest (Tour 2, see page 23) offers highly enjoyable cycling on trails through the woodland.

Beaches and swimming

Norfolk and Suffolk's coastline is fringed by numerous beaches, many of them, especially on the Norfolk Coast, are long and sandy. Resorts

On the beach at Wells-next-the-Sea

range from the archetypal bucket-and-spade destinations with sticks of rock and amusement arcades to unspoilt little hamlets by the sea where the main activity is catching crabs. On the Norfolk coast you'll find huge expanses of flat sand at Brancaster, Holkham and Wells-next-the-Sea. Many of the beaches along this coast shelve very gradually, which means wading out some way before you find water deep enough for swimming. And because of the vast expanses of sand revealed at low tide it can be up to a mile (1.6km) even for a paddle. Visitors should be aware of fast incoming tides

One toe in the sea

If you're used to indoor pools or Mediterranean waters you'll find the sea temperatures on the chilly side, even in mid-summer. Most beach-goers do no more than paddle, leaving the seas delightfully crowd-free for serious swimmers. Favourite activities for youngsters are fishing around in pools when the tide goes out and catching crabs – usually with a piece of bacon tied on string. Walberswick and Blakeney are two of the most popular crabbing spots.

There are some great crabbing spots along the coast

A river cruise in Suffolk on board the *Lady Florence*

and rip currents. Lifeguards operate at main resorts during the peak season. Cromer, Sheringham, East and West Runton, Mundesley and Sea Palling are all Blue Flag beaches.

Suffolk's coast is wilder with pebbly beaches as well as some sandy ones with dunes. One of the best beaches is at Southwold, holder of a Blue Flag award.

Leisure centres and lidos

If the sea water is too cool there are always the leisure centres and the lidos. Hunstanton has the Alive Oasis centre (tel: 01485 534 227; www.alivewest norfolk.co.uk), and Great Yarmouth's Marina Centre (tel: 01493 851 521; www.marinalc.co.uk) has a pool, wave machine, slide and fun sessions.

Beccles Lido (tel: 01502 713 297; www.beccleslido.com; end May–early Sept), next to the River Waveney, is a traditional, good-sized outdoor pool, heated to 80ºF (27ºC), with a 1-metre (3ft) springboard and a slide at the shallow end. There are separate heated toddler and paddling pools, and grassy areas for sunbathing and picnics.

Boating

The Norfolk Broads offers all kinds of boating opportunities, whether you're a seasoned sailor or have never been on a boat in your life. You can stay on a motor boat or sailing cruiser, hire a canoe or rowing boat, take a cruise with live commentary and lunch on board or a wildlife trip on a little electric boat (see page 48) through scenic waterways. In Suffolk one of the loveliest boat trips is the river cruise from Orford on the *Lady Florence* (tel: 01473 558 712; www.lady-florence. co.uk), offering brunch, lunch, dinner and sunset supper cruises (maximum 12 people). The boat sails year-round, with a cosy coal fire in winter, and the chance to see the elegant avocet.

Hiring a boat requires no qualifications – provided you're not sailing. Hoseasons (tel: 0844 8847 1112; www.hoseasons.co.uk) has a large choice of cruisers, from budget boats to chic contemporary vessels, and five main departure points from which to explore the Broads. BarnesBrinkcraft (tel: 01603 782 625; www.barnesbrinkcraft.co.uk) rent out canoes and diverse leisure crafts which can be rented for an hour, half a day or a whole day.

Sailing and surfing

The north Norfolk coast and the Norfolk Broads are both popular for sailing, and Blakeney is the favourite spot for those with their own boat. Based in Ludham on the Norfolk Broads, Hunter's Yard (tel: 01692 678 263; www.huntersyard.co.uk) offer a variety of Royal Yachting Association Qualified sailing courses and, for those with some experience, there are traditional wooden sailing keelboats (no engine or electric power) for hire. Cromer is a popular spot for surfers, just by the pier. You can learn the skill or improve your technique at the Glide Surf School (tel: 07966 392 227; www.glidesurfschool.co.uk).

Canoeing and kayaking

Canoeing is a wonderful way to discover the Broads and it is suitable for all the family, including young children. Canadian canoes usually carry up to three adults. Full instructions are given and buoyancy aids provided. The Canoe Man (tel: 07873 748 408;

Sailing off Blakeney Point

www.thecanoeman.com) in Wroxham hires out canoes and kayaks, and also offers guided canoe trails, overnight canoe trails, wild swimming and bush-craft courses. To explore the Norfolk coast by kayak, Hunstanton Kayaks (tel: 07810 188 165; www.hunstanton kayaks.co.uk) have craft for hire and also run trips for all abilities. If you're lucky you might see some seals.

Place your bets

Newmarket, Great Yarmouth and Fakenham all have race courses. Newmarket is easily the most famous with two race courses – the Rowley Mile and the July Course. Meetings are held between April and October (visit www.thejockeyclub.co.uk/ newmarket for information). Great Yarmouth stadium is East Anglia's premier greyhound racing venue with races Monday, Wednesday and Saturday evenings. It offers grandstand seating, a restaurant and two bars. Bookings required (www.yarmouthstadium.co.uk).

The thrill of the race

Fishing

With its rivers and shallow lakes the Norfolk Broads is one of the best locations in the region for fishing, either from boats or angling platforms along the river banks. The Broads support a variety of freshwater fish, including roach, bream, perch, tench, eels and pike, as well as estuarine species such as flounders, sea bass and grey mullet. The coarse fishing season runs from mid-June to mid-March and a current Environment Agency licence (www.environment-agency.gov.uk) is required.

The High Lodge activity centre on the Suffolk Coast (see page 119) offers coarse fishing in two lakes, with carp (up to 20lbs), tench (up to 4lbs), roach, perch and rudd. A reasonably priced day ticket or short break pass are available. Fishing licence required.

Golf

Norfolk and Suffolk have around 60 courses between them, catering for players of all abilities. For a list, visit www.golftoday.co.uk. In Norfolk, the Royal West Norfolk (or Brancaster as it is known), Hunstanton, King's Lynn, Royal Cromer and Sheringham rank among the best; in Suffolk, top courses are Aldeburgh, Thorpeness, Stowmarket, Woodbridge and the Royal Worlington at Bury St Edmunds and Newmarket.

There are plenty of courses that are safe and fun for junior golfers to learn and play, such as Bawburgh (www.bawburgh.com) in Norfolk, which has won awards for encouraging juniors and beginners.

Horseriding

Woodlands, beaches and bridle paths make for pleasurable horseriding in the region and tourist information centres have details of riding schools and centres. The Squirrelwood Equestrian Centre (tel: 07586 292 149; www.squirrelwood.co.uk) situated between Holt and Sheringham is one of several Norfolk horseriding centres, catering for all ages and abilities. In Suffolk, the Pakefield Riding School (tel: 01502

Canoeing at Blakeney

Fishing at Oulton Broad

572 257; www.pakefieldridingschool.co.uk), established in 1946, offers lessons and rides to the beach and local woods.

Activity and theme parks

Elveden Forest in Suffolk is home to one of the UK's five Center Parcs, (tel: 03448 267 723; www.centerparcs.co.uk), the award-winning holiday villages for weekends and short breaks. Lodges in the woodland sleep 2–8 and activities are abundant: zip wires through the forest, canoeing on the lake, go-karting, roller skating, fencing, fitness classes or just splashing around in the Subtropical Swimming Paradise. Activities are organized for children of all ages but there's plenty for parents to do too.

Easton Farm Park (near Woodbridge; tel: 01728 746 475; www.eastonfarmpark.co.uk) is a big hit with children who have the chance to meet Suffolk Punch carthorses, ride ponies and see baby lambs and donkey foals. In addition are barrel bug and family train rides, craft workshop and two indoor play barns.

Go Ape! (High Lodge, Thetford Forest; tel: 0845 643 9215; www.go ape.co.uk) is an award-winning forest adventure, with zip wires, Tarzan swings and a variety of obstacles. The Tree Top Junior is designed for younger Tarzans.

Pleasurewood Hills (Leisure Way, Lowestoft; tel: 01502 586 000; www.pleasurewoodhills.com; April–Oct) is the biggest theme park in the East of England, offering over 20 family rides, along with half a dozen scarier thrill rides, including the region's largest rollercoaster, Wipeout. Booking online saves you around 10 percent and season passes are available.

BeWILDerwood

By far the best theme park in the region is BeWILDerwood (Hoveton; tel: 01692 633 033; www.bewilderwood.co.uk), a great breakthrough for sustainable UK family tourism. It is a magical playground of wobbly wires, tree houses, boat rides and jungle bridges, with weird and wonderful forest folk. Everything is built from sustainable wood and some 14,000 broad-leaf trees have been planted. A wonderful family day out which harks back to old-fashioned childhood adventures.

There's fun for children and adults alike at BeWILDerwood

Themed Holidays

From bushcraft workshops to luxury spas, a wide variety of holidays and activities are on offer in Norfolk and Suffolk.

Art and photography

Where better to attend a residential art course than the heart of Constable country, right on the Essex/Suffolk border. Dedham Hall (tel: 01206 323 027; www.dedhamhall.co.uk) is a delightful country house hotel set in peaceful gardens with a spacious art studio. Paint in the countryside that inspired John Constable. Courses can range from a few days to a full week.

In a beautiful atmospheric setting at Pin Mill on the Shotley Peninsula on the Suffolk coast, Anthony Cullen (tel: 01473 780 130; www.photographic day.com) runs one- and two-day photography courses for individuals or small groups, teaching basic techniques or more advanced skills.

Learn art techniques and have fun on a weekend art course with Nicola Slattery (tel: 01986 788 853; www.nicolaslattery.com), who has been running short art courses for over 20 years. Themes are likely to be printmaking, art from imagination and painting with acrylics. All levels are catered for and materials are provided along with buffet lunches. Courses take place in a pretty spot in southern Norfolk and for accommodation there are excellent farmhouses, B&Bs and old country inns nearby.

Cycling

Cycle Breaks (tel: 01449 721 555; www.cyclebreaks.com/cycling-in-eng land) has been organizing self-guided cycling tours since 1991. Cyclists just follow their maps and have their luggage taken ahead to their accommodation – usually comfortable and characterful B&Bs. There are themed itineraries and plenty of good recommendations for coffee stops, pubs and eating out.

Family holidays

South of Lowestoft, Pontins Pakefield (tel: 0871 222 0201; www.pontins. com) offers fun-packed family breaks

Cycling through the Norfolk countryside

(and ones for adults only) throughout the year. Expect simple modern accommodation and endless activities including quad bikes, pitch and putt, arts and crafts, bike hire, trampolining, line dancing, snooker and bingo.

Music

Ace Cultural Tours (tel: 01223 841 055; www.aceculturaltours.co.uk) organizes four-day breaks to Aldeburgh, centred around the famous Aldeburgh Festival in June. Tours include concerts, lectures and local sightseeing.

Nature conservation

Stay in luxury tents amongst the trees at Secret Meadows Luxury Camping, (tel: 01394 382 992; www.secretmeadows. co.uk) near Woodbridge. By staying at this 115-acre (47-hectare) wildlife site, you are supporting the nature conservation charity that owns the site.

Outdoor activities

Outdoor activities on offer at Iken Barns (tel: 01728 688 899; www.iken barns.com) include cycling or paddling on a kayak to Snape or Aldeburgh. Also on offer are pony camps, bring-your-own-horse holidays, lessons in the indoor school or hacking in the local forest. Weekend retreat breaks also available. It is advisable to book well in advance.

Not to be confused with one of the same name in Thetford Forest, the High Lodge activity centre west of Dunwich (just off the A12) offers activity breaks with clay pigeon and air rifle shooting, archery, fishing, golf on the nine-hole course and the new activity footgolf, with accommodation in lake-view lodges (tel: 01986 784 347; www.highlodge.co.uk).

Pampering

Escape from the stresses of everyday life by booking into one of the region's

A guided tour of Flatford Mill

Beauty Spas. A number of hotels in the region, particularly in Suffolk, offer treatments: *The Lifehouse Spa and Hotel* in Thorpe-le-Soken (tel: 01255 860 050; www.lifehouse.co.uk), *Ufford Park Hotel* at Woodbridge (tel: 01394 383 555; www.uffordpark.co.uk) and *Hintlesham Hall Hotel* near Ipswich (tel: 01473 652 334; www.hintlesham hall.co.uk). In Norfolk, the Beauty Spa at *The Hoste*, Burnham Market (see page 125) is a peaceful retreat in a chic hotel and the *Congham Hall Hotel & Spa* (tel: 01485 600 250; www.conghamhallhotel.co.uk) near King's Lynn is set in gorgeous grounds.

Walking

British and Irish Walking Holidays (tel: 01242 254 353; www.britishand irishwalks.com) offers easy guided walks through Constable Country, a beautiful region of water-meadows, villages and churches, as immortalized by Britain's great landscape painter, John Constable. Walks include Dedham, the Stour River to Flatford Mill, East Bergholt, where Constable was born, and the villages of Stoke-by-Nayland and Nayland. B&B accommodation is at Dedham and Nayland.

Practical Information

Getting there

By road

There are good links with London and the Midlands, though neither Norfolk nor Suffolk has a motorway. From London, the South East of England, ferry ports and the Channel Tunnel the major roads to East Anglia are the M11, A11, A12, A140 and A14. The fastest route to Suffolk from London is the A12 for Ipswich, then the A12 or A14 for the rest of the county. For Norwich and Norfolk take the M11 and the A11. From the Midlands and the North the region is served by the A14, A11, A47, A17 and A1.

By rail

For national rail enquiries visit www.nationalrail.co.uk (tel: 03457 484 950, lines open 24 hours). Abellio Greater Anglia (tel: 0345 600 7245; www.abelliogreateranglia.co.uk) runs services from London King's Cross to Cambridge, Ely and King's Lynn, and from London Liverpool Street to Colchester, Ipswich and Norwich.

Connecting services are available from the Midlands, north of England and Scotland via Peterborough. Book early for the best fares.

By bus

For national coach information contact National Express (tel: 08717 818 181, lines open 24 hours; www.nationalexpress.com). Coaches travel daily to East Anglia from London (Victoria Coach Station), the Midlands and the Southeast.

By air

The main airports for the region are Stansted (tel: 0844 335 1803; www.stanstedairport.com) and Norwich (tel: 01603 411 923; www.norwichairport.co.uk), which is just 4 miles (7km) northwest of the city centre. Both are linked by road and rail to Heathrow, Gatwick, Luton and the East Midlands airports.

By sea

Car and passenger ferries operate between the Hook of Holland and

Suffolk farmland

There is no shortage of places to visit in Norfolk and Suffolk

Harwich with Stena Line (tel: 08447 707 070; www.stenaline.co.uk).

By bicycle

East Anglia is on the Sustrans National Cycle Network (tel: 0117 926 8893; www.sustrans.org.uk) Hull to Harwich (Route 1), the North Sea Cycle Route and National Route 11, which connects King's Lynn with Cambridge.

Getting around

Bus and coach

Norfolk and Suffolk are served by several operators including Anglian Bus (tel: 01502 711 109; www.anglian bus.co.uk) and First Group (tel: 0871 200 2233; www.firstgroup.com). Local services around the Ipswich, Stowmarket and Bury St Edmunds area are run by Galloway (tel: 01449 766 323; www.travel-galloway.com). The Norfolk Coast hopper bus service (see page 122) operates a regular timetable between King's Lynn and Cromer.

Cycling

Cycling is an ideal way to discover the countryside. There are numerous designated cycle routes and detailed information at tourist information offices and visitor centres. Ordnance Survey maps are invaluable for cycling (and public footpaths), marking on-road and traffic-free cycle routes, both national and regional.

Rail

For timetables, ticket prices and other information visit National Rail Enquiries (tel: 03457 484 950; www.nationalrail.co.uk) or Abellio Greater Anglia (tel: 0345 600 7245; www.abelliogreateranglia.co.uk). From Norwich the Bittern and Wherry Lines (www.bitternline.com and www.wherrylines.org.uk) operate services to the coast via the Broads.

Driving

Driving can be slow, especially along the coast or getting to the coast on summer weekends and holidays. The 'A' roads link the main centres. There are some very narrow lanes connecting inland villages but driving is rarely a problem.

Car hire

Most car hire companies will only rent to 21–75 year olds, with at least a year's experience of driving. In some cases the minimum age is 23. Shop around for special weekend and holiday rates.
Avis tel: 0808 284 0014; www.avis.co.uk.
Enterprise tel: 0800 800 227; www.enterprise.co.uk.
Europcar tel: 0871 384 9900; www.europcar.co.uk.

Parking

Parking in most town centres is discouraged, but car parks are normally located within easy walking distances of the centre.

Going green

In Norfolk you can board the Bittern Line railway which runs from Norwich to Cromer or Sheringham or jump on to the Coasthopper bus (tel: 01553 776 980; www.coasthopper. co.uk) to travel between King's Lynn and Cromer. This is one of the UK's most popular rural bus services, normally operating May–Sept daily up to half-hourly, but less frequently in spring and autumn and especially winter. The combination of the Norfolk Coast Path and the Coasthopper means leaving the car behind is an easy option.

Suffolk County Council has an excellent website (www.discover suffolk.org.uk) which promotes cycling, walking and outdoor activities, with interactive maps and downloadable walking guides and cycle maps, plus information on country parks, picnic spots, wildlife sites and bird reserves.

Facts for the visitor

Travellers with disabilities

An increasing number of hotels and restaurants have access. At nature reserves the boardwalks are normally wheelchair friendly. There are accessible public toilets and Blue Badge parking bays across the region. Open Britain (tel: 0845 124 9971; www.openbritain.net), a website managed by the Tourism For All UK charity, provides information on accessible holiday and travel.

Emergencies

In an absolute emergency call 999 for fire, ambulance or police. Call the National Health Service number 111 when you need medical help but it is less urgent than 999. Otherwise take a taxi to the nearest casualty department of a hospital.

Entertainment

Most of the entertainment is concentrated in main towns and

Cyclists in Suffolk; you can find routes and interactive maps on the county council website

End-of-the-pier entertainment, Great Yarmouth

resorts, which offer theatre and concerts. Summer festivals take place across both counties. Norwich has a good choice of drama, music or dance at the Theatre Royal or Norwich Arts Centre, and comedy at the Norwich Playhouse. Cromer on the north Norfolk coast has great variety-style shows at the end of its pier. Bury St Edmunds is home to the intimate little Theatre Royal and The Apex music and entertainment venue. Check out what's on from the tourist information websites: www.visitnorfolk.com and www.visitsuffolk.com.

LGBTQ travellers

The LGBTQ scene is mainly in the cities and towns. In Norwich, *The Castle* (1 Spitalfields; tel: 01603 768 886; www.thecastle-pub.com) is billed as Norwich's Premier Gay Bar & Club. *The Loft Nr1* is a gay nightclub with a late-night bar, terrace and dance floor, Thurs–Sat only.

Opening hours

Shops generally open Mon–Sat 9am–5.30pm, although smaller towns and villages may have a half-day closing one day a week. Large shopping centres are likely to have one evening of late-night shopping and an increasing number of shops are open on Sundays. Most banks open Mon–Fri 9.30am–4.30/5pm with Saturday banking common in shopping areas. Most pubs will take last drink orders at 11pm Mon–Sat and at 10.30pm on Sundays.

Tourist information

Main tourist information centres provide (not necessarily free) pamphlets on walks and cycle trails, maps of the area and information on local attractions and events.

Bury St Edmunds, The Apex, Charter Square; tel: 01284 758 101; www.visit-burystedmunds.co.uk.

Cambridge, Peas Hill; tel: 01223 791 500; www.visitcambridge.org.

Cromer, Louden Road; tel: 01263 512 497; www.visitnorfolk.co.uk.

Great Yarmouth, 25 Marine Parade; tel: 01493 846 346; www.great-yarmouth.co.uk.

King's Lynn, The Custom House; tel: 01553 763 044; www.visitnorfolk.com.

Norwich, The Forum; tel: 01603 213 999; www.visitnorwich.co.uk.

Wroxham, 10 Norwich Road; tel: 0845 496 177; e-mail: info@Norfolk BroadsTIC.com.

Accommodation

From quirky B&Bs and boathouses to country manor houses and luxury hotels, Norfolk and Suffolk cater for all tastes. Wherever you are staying it's wise to book ahead in the summer, especially from mid-July to the end of August, and at Easter. Many hotels offer special weekend and low-season breaks between October and April.

To find the best deals, book online. Most hotels include breakfast in their rates. In some of the most sought-after spots, especially on the coast, two nights will be the minimum at weekends. Bed-and-breakfasts or guesthouses, quite often in farmhouses, can offer more character and better value than hotels, with excellent home-cooked breakfasts and owners who are a mine of information on the local area.

One of the sumptuous rooms at the *Ickworth Hotel*, Bury St Edmunds

The region offers abundant campsites, from no-frills family-run places to 'glamping' (glamorous camping), where you have the choice of yurts, tepees, caravans, bell tents and shepherds' huts, usually on ecofriendly sites in lovely locations.

The Visit Suffolk (www.visit suffolk.co.uk) and Visit Norfolk (www.visitnorfolk.co.uk) websites have detailed information on accommodation. Other useful sources include Norfolk Bed and Breakfast (www.norfolk-bed-and-breakfast.co.uk) and The Suffolk Coast (www.suffolkcoast.co.uk).

There are numerous self-catering cottages. Norfolk Country Cottages (www.norfolkcottages.co.uk) and Suffolk Cottage Holidays (www.suffolkcottageholidays. com) have a wide selection of self-catering accommodation. For boating holidays, Hoseasons (www.hoseasons.co.uk) is one of the biggest operators.

Hotels

The price bands below are a guideline for the cost of a standard en-suite double room and breakfast for two people in high season.

£££ = over £250
££ = £150–250
£ = under £150

Aldeburgh
Brudenell
The Parade; tel: 01728 452 071; www.brudenellhotel.co.uk.
The relaxing seaside atmosphere, panoramic views and good food draw many regulars to this 4-star contemporary hotel. Guest rooms are decorated in calming colours inspired by the coast. ££

The Wentworth

Wentworth Road; tel: 01728 452 312;
www.wentworth-aldeburgh.com.
In the hands of the same family since
1920, this is an appealing traditional
hotel overlooking the beach. There are
spacious sea-view lounges, sea-facing
gardens and roaring log fires off-
season. Good food too. ££

Blakeney
Blakeney Hotel

The Quay; tel: 01263 740 797;
www.blakeneyhotel.co.uk.
Family-run, friendly hotel with a great
quayside location overlooking the
estuary and salt marshes. It's worth
paying the extra for full estuary views.
Restaurant, swimming pool, spa bath,
sauna and mini-gym. ££

Burnham Market
The Hoste

The Green; tel: 01328 738 777;
www.thehoste.com.
Overlooking The Green in the
lovely Georgian village of Burnham
Market, this has evolved over the
years from a country inn with half a
dozen simple rooms to the boutique
hotel of today. Guest rooms, some
of which are in village annexes, are
individually decorated and range from
the traditional (including room No. 5
where Nelson once stayed) to 'Divine'
rooms with stylish contemporary decor
and luxury bathrooms. The staff are
friendly and attentive and the on-site
beauty spa offers luxury pampering
and relaxation. The garden restaurant
is delightful in summer. ££

Bury St Edmunds
Ickworth Hotel

Horringer; tel: 01284 735 350;
www.ickworthhotel.co.uk.
A deluxe hotel, with self-catering as
well as guest rooms, occupying the
east wing of Ickworth House (see page

Cley Windmill – accommodation with a difference

79). It's child friendly with family
dining, a crèche, a pool, bikes to hire
and 1,800 acres (728 hectares) of
parkland for letting off steam. Check
for special family deals. £££

Cambridge
Gonville Hotel

Gonville Place; tel: 01223 366 611;
www.gonvillehotel.co.uk.
Just a short stroll away from the centre
of Cambridge, the Gonville has the
added bonus of overlooking Parker's
Piece, which comprises 25 acres (10
hectares) of parkland. The service is
friendly and efficient and the rooms
well appointed. ££

Varsity Hotel & Spa

Thompson's Lane, off Bridge
Street; tel: 01223 306 030;
www.thevarsityhotel.co.uk.
The Varsity is probably the most stylish
place to sleep in the city. It boasts a
rooftop garden with views over the
colleges, an impressive restaurant and a
beautiful spa and gym. £££

Cley-next-the-Sea
Cley Windmill

Cley Windmill; tel: 01263 740 209;
www.cleywindmill.co.uk.

Oozing charm and character, this is a renovated 18th-century mill with great views of the salt marshes and sea, and a friendly, private-home atmosphere. ££

Coltishall
The Norfolk Mead Hotel
Church Loke; tel: 01603 737 531; www.norfolkmead.co.uk.
Six miles (10km) from Norwich, on the edge of the Broads, this lovely country hotel is the perfect place to relax. Gardens extend to the banks of the River Bure, and include a walled garden, lush lawns and private lake. Guest rooms are light, airy and restful, and the award-winning restaurant makes the most of produce from local farms and markets. The breakfasts here are a great way to start the day. ££

Lavenham
The Swan at Lavenham
High Street; tel: 01787 247 477; www.theswanatlavenham.co.uk.
You cannot fail to be impressed by the stunning 15th-century Swan. It is totally in harmony with the beautiful medieval village and although traditional, it offers luxury and indulgence. There's a first-class restaurant and relaxing spa. ££

Norwich
The Assembly House
Theatre Street; tel: 01603 626 402; www.assemblyhousenorwich.co.uk.
Choose from 11 stylish rooms in this beautiful Georgian house, six of which have their own little garden or terrace. Each room is individually decorated to a very high standard and some have four-poster beds. Splendour is maintained in the public rooms, where you can eat first-class meals in stunning surroundings. ££
The Maids Head
20 Tombland; tel: 01603 209 955; www.maidsheadhotel.co.uk.

This historic and quirky hotel has a superb location opposite the cathedral. It goes back 800 years, and claims to be the oldest hotel in Britain. The Black Prince and Catherine of Aragon are among its famous guests. Rooms vary hugely in size and style. The old ones have far more character than those in the modern extension. Street rooms can be noisy. Free parking, good restaurant. £

Southwold
The Crown
High Street; tel: 01502 722 275; www.thecrownsouthwold.co.uk.
This old inn is owned by Adnams Brewery so you know the beer will be good. There are 14 rooms in contemporary style and a popular bar-restaurant. ££

Wells-next-the-Sea
The Crown Hotel
The Buttlands; tel: 01328 710 209; www.crownhotelnorfolk.co.uk.
A former coaching inn on a lovely leafy square, this boutique hotel has 20 stylish rooms. It is owned by celebrity chef, Chris Coubrough, so you can be assured of top-notch cuisine (see page 42). £

The Swan at Lavenham

Index

Credits

Rough Guide Staycations Norfolk & Suffolk
Editor: Zara Sekhavati
Authors: Susie Boulton and Hilary Weston
Head of DTP and Pre-Press: Rebeka Davies
Picture Editor: Tom Smyth
Head of Publishing: Sarah Clark

Photo credits: BeWILDerwood 7M, 46B, 117B; Bigstock 96T; Carys Lavin/Latitude 63B; Corrie Wingate/Apa Publications 6MC, 7TR, 36, 37, 46T, 58, 59, 62T, 76, 90T, 113T, 115T; Getty Images 4/5, 74/75T; iStock 7MR, 7M, 56TL, 56ML, 71T, 72T, 81B, 89, 100T, 115B, 126; Luxury Family Hotels 124; Matt Jolly/Aldeburgh Festival 74TL, 74ML; Public domain 108T; Shutterstock 1, 48, 51, 122; Simon Talbot-Hurn/REX/Shutterstock 64; Sylvaine Poitau/Apa Publications 6ML, 6MC, 6ML, 7T, 7BR, 8/9, 9, 10, 11, 12, 13, 14, 15, 16, 17, 18, 19B, 19T, 20T, 20B, 22, 23, 24T, 24B, 25, 27, 28, 29, 30B, 30T, 31, 32, 33, 34T, 34B, 38, 39T, 39B, 40T, 40B, 41T, 41B, 43, 44, 44/45, 47T, 47B, 50, 52, 53, 54, 56/57T, 60, 61T, 61B, 62B, 63T, 66, 67, 68, 69T, 69B, 70, 71B, 72B, 77, 78T, 78B, 79T, 79B, 80T, 80B, 81T, 82B, 82T, 83, 85, 86T, 86B, 88/89T, 88B, 90B, 91, 92, 92/93, 94, 94/95T, 95B, 96B, 98, 99, 100B, 102TL, 102ML, 102/103T, 104, 105, 106, 107T, 107B, 108B, 110/111, 112, 113B, 114, 116, 117T, 118, 119, 120, 121, 123, 125
Cover credit: Sunset over Brograve Mill on the Norfolk Broads **Shutterstock**

Contact Us

Every effort has been made to provide accurate information in this publication, but changes are inevitable. The publisher cannot be held responsible for any resulting loss, inconvenience or injury sustained by any traveller as a result of information or advice contained in the guide. We would appreciate it if readers would call our attention to any errors or outdated information, or if you feel we've left something out. Please send your comments with the subject line "**Rough Guide Staycations Norfolk & Suffolk Update**" to mail@uk.roughguides.com.

First Edition 2021

Printed in Poland

Contains Land-Form Panorama Contours & Meridian 2 and OS Street View data © Crown copyright and database right.

Distribution

UK, Ireland and Europe: Apa Publications (UK) Ltd; sales@roughguides.com
United States and Canada: Ingram Publisher Services; ips@ingramcontent.com
Australia and New Zealand: Booktopia; retailer@booktopia.com.au
Worldwide: Apa Publications (UK) Ltd; sales@roughguides.com

Special Sales, Content Licensing and CoPublishing

Rough Guides can be purchased in bulk quantities at discounted prices. We can create special editions, personalised jackets and corporate imprints tailored to your needs. sales@roughguides.com; http://roughguides.com